Channeled Teachings

ℱREEDOM NOW

Transform Your Life
Experiences into
Miraculous Moments

PATTI FIELDS

ARS METAPHYSICA

an imprint of Sunbury Press, Inc.
Mechanicsburg, PA USA

ARS METAPHYSICA

an imprint of Sunbury Press, Inc.
Mechanicsburg, PA USA

For information about special discounts for bulk purchases, please contact Sunbury Press Orders Dept. at (855) 338-8359 or orders@sunburypress.com.

To request one of our authors for speaking engagements or book signings, please contact Sunbury Press Publicity Dept. at publicity@sunburypress.com.

FIRST ARS METAPHYSICA EDITION: December 2024

Set in Adobe Garamond | Interior design by Crystal Devine | Cover by Lawrence Knorr | Edited by Lawrence Knorr.

Publisher's Cataloging-in-Publication Data
Names: Fields, Patti, author.
Title: Freedom now : transform your life experiences into miraculous moments / Patti Fields.
Description: First trade paperback edition. | Mechanicsburg, PA : Ars Metaphysica, 2024.
Summary: Patti Fields' spirit guide, Neshea imparts practical and profound teachings to release fear and distress and experience love and connection in every present moment—even the most challenging ones. Topics include Divine purpose, relationships, decisions, change, abundance, expanded states of consciousness, and manifestation.
Identifiers: ISBN : 979-8-88819-293-1 (softcover).
Subjects: BODY, MIND & SPIRIT / Healing / Prayer & Spiritual | BODY, MIND & SPIRIT / Dreams | SELF-HELP / Spiritual.

Designed in the USA
0 1 1 2 3 5 8 13 21 34 55

For the Love of Books!

To my spirit guide, Neshea—

Your teachings are a beacon of light, especially during challenging times.

I am forever grateful for our dream encounter.

Also by Patti Fields

Dreaming Miracles—Spiritual Messages That Help and Heal

CHANNELED TEACHINGS
A Lightworker's Guide to Fulfilling Your Destiny
A Guide to Aligning with the Source of Healing
Special Instructions for the Role of the Healer
Your Role in Co-Creating
A Guide to Communicating with the Spiritual Realm
Navigating Life Transitions, Changes, and Transformations

ↄ

For purchasing information visit Patti's website:
www.pattifields.com

Contents

A Note from the Author — ix

Introduction — 1
    The Dream That Started It All — 3
    An Encouraging Message to Me from Neshea — 8
    A Message to the Reader from Neshea — 9

PART I: The Universal Answer — 11
    Messages from February 5 to March 8 — 13

PART II: Dissolving Difficulties — 89
    Messages from March 9 to March 26 — 91

PART III: Relationships — 119
    Messages from March 27 to April 6 — 121

PART IV: Special Topics — 145
    Change — 147
    Manifestation — 150
    Abundance — 154
    Love — 157
    Doubt — 159

Concluding Messages — 163
    The Power of Love — 165
    Experiencing Heaven on Earth — 167
    One Last Question . . . — 169
    Neshea's Final Words — 171

Reflections and Revelations 173

Thank You 175

References 176

About the Author 177

A Note from the Author

Know thyself.

—INSCRIPTION AT THE TEMPLE OF APOLLO
(DELPHI)

WHY DON'T we have the relationship we desire? Why do we lack abundance? How can we be free of fear? How do we obtain true peace? What relieves suffering? What's our life's purpose? As a spiritual teacher, I was often asked these questions by students wanting to improve their lives. As a spiritual student, when I asked these questions, the answers came through dreams and visions.

Over the years, I have shared my dream and vision messages during presentations, workshops, classes, and retreats. The impact of these messages and the growing interest in my dreams and visions inspired me to write my first book, *Dreaming Miracles—Spiritual Messages That Help and Heal.*

While completing *Dreaming Miracles*, an unexpected event occurred. A spiritual dream introduced me to one of my spirit guides, Neshea. The following morning, I surprisingly received the first of over fifty channeled messages from Neshea. His words were so profound and compelling that it was clear they would be helpful to others. I immediately began transcribing the messages to share them in my new book, *Freedom Now.*

Both *Freedom Now* and *Dreaming Miracles* address the common challenge of feeling trapped in experiences of fear, pain, lack, insecurity, unworthiness, loneliness, and guilt.

Dreaming Miracles shares spiritual answers that, when applied to universal life challenges, result in breakthroughs. *Freedom Now* offers teachings on the transformational power of the present moment. Through Neshea's practical and profound messages, we learn how to release our deepest fears and discover our spiritual treasures in every present moment.

Love, appreciation, and genuine helpfulness were the energies that guided me while scribing Neshea's teachings. These energies are the source of the messages, and I share them with you in the same spirit they were given. I hope that both books become a resource for you to experience authentic freedom and true happiness in your life.

Introduction

Will you not answer the call of love with joy?

A COURSE IN MIRACLES

The Dream That Started It All

O N T H E evening of Monday, February 4, 2019, I had a spiritual dream. This experience was nothing new for me. Over the years, I have received hundreds of transformative dreams that provided profound answers to life's challenges. This particular dream was different, though. In this dream, I connected with one of my spirit guides, and the information I received changed everything . . .

My heart pounds with anticipation as I approach the large conference room. It's been ages since I've taken a class, and I'm excited to be a student again. I eagerly cross the threshold, enter the room, and survey my surroundings.

Hundreds of chairs face a stage at the north end of the room. Participants mill around the rows of chairs, looking for a seat. I scurry to claim an unoccupied chair in the last row but quickly change my mind when I realize that I won't be able to hear or see anything from the back of the room. I hurry to the stage and consider sitting in the first row. This location doesn't seem right either. Scanning the room for other options, I spot several empty rows of chairs to the far right of the stage. I wander over and take a seat. Satisfied, I excitedly wait for the teacher to appear.

I delight in the prospect of learning something new. I know a little bit about the subject matter, but I am not proficient in it. I will definitely need to take notes. I remind myself to buy a notebook.

The quiet murmur of voices shifts my attention away from these thoughts toward the small clusters of students engaged in friendly conversations. That is when I see him for the first time.

His bright, colorful robes and headdress catch my eye. Yet, it is his warmth, kindness, and jovial manner that draw me in. Propelled by a strong urge to speak to him, I purposefully leave my seat, walk over, and introduce myself. He smiles, repositions two chairs so that they face each other, and, with a friendly gesture, motions for me to take a seat. Draping his arm casually over a chair, he seems content to talk with me as long as I want. We chat about trivial matters. He giggles at something I say. His lighthearted, whimsical manner is endearing. Yet, I am not fooled by his casual and boyish demeanor. It is obvious to me that he is a very wise man.

As we continue discussing inconsequential topics, I have a silent epiphany. His wisdom and consistent state of peace and joy are the result of learning through life experiences rather than through meditative practice. Struck by an intense desire to learn all he knows, I blurt out, "Can I interview you?" Easily adjusting to the change in tone and topic of our conversation, he smiles and replies, "Of course."

What happens next is difficult to describe. Slowly waking up from the dream, and with my eyes still closed, I see four words parade across my mind. A split second later, my radio alarm goes off, and I hear the DJ speak the EXACT same four words! Slowly, it dawns on me that an extraordinary phenomenon has just occurred.

As I lie there, savoring the moment, a question pops into my mind. *Is this what it is like to receive a spiritual message while awake?* I pause and consider the possibility. My dreams and visions have been consistent, valuable resources for insights and guidance. Why would last night's dream and this unusual event be any different? Encouraged, I get out of bed, retrieve my digital recorder from the file cabinet, scramble through the bookshelf for a notebook, and take a seat. I write down a simple question: "What would you share with us now?" The instant I close my eyes, words appear in my mind. I speak the words into the recorder so I can transcribe them later.

The interview process has begun . . .

CHANNELING – AN AMAZING EXPERIENCE

Life is a series of events that, when strung together, make up a story that can be quite marvelous. Some of the events are familiar, and some moments are a complete surprise.

When I turned on the recorder each morning, I did not know what would happen next. This experience was both exciting and uncomfortable. Regardless, I continued to listen because I was intrigued by this new way of receiving messages and wanted to glean as much information as possible from this higher source of knowledge. Who wouldn't want to know more about how to use life experiences to gain freedom and happiness?

Each channeled message was a step into the unknown. For instance, when the last message of Part I was received, I was surprised to learn there was a Part II, a Part III, and additional teachings on specific themes. Some of the messages were provided out of sequence. For example, the "Message to the Reader" was the last message I received, and the special topic messages were given after the concluding messages. Having no prior knowledge of the teachings or outcome helped me to remain open and receive Neshea's instructions.

Initially, I needed a way to distinguish between my thoughts and the channeled message. To help me, I was given the word "love" to indicate the beginning of the channeled message. I also found it helpful to ask a question to prepare my mind to receive a message. As I became more comfortable with the unknown, the need to ask a question naturally faded away. At the end of each message, I expressed gratitude because all the messages touched my heart deeply. Saying "thank you" was a natural response to what I had received.

Some of the messages included a present moment mantra and a morning and bedtime mantra. These were given in response to my request for a thought to help me remain focused and consistent in my practice. You might find these mantras helpful, as well. Periodically, I would receive messages that addressed a specific topic, a personal life experience, my curiosity, or the meaning of a nighttime dream. These messages are included in Part IV and are titled so they can be easily referenced.

It was not always convenient for me to sit quietly and receive messages in the early morning hours. Sometimes, I needed to fulfill a previously scheduled commitment or respond to an unexpected event. I wondered if my inability to begin my day in silence would stop the flow of messages. This worry was unnecessary. Regardless of the time of day, the messages continued without effort whenever I was ready to listen. What a joy to learn that no matter how much time passes, there is always a response to our call for help.

A few weeks after I began scribing the teachings, I traveled to care for a family member recovering from surgery. Troubled by the abrupt halt to receiving messages, I wondered, *Would I lose the love, peace, comfort, and certainty I experienced when connecting with Neshea?* I decided that during the hiatus, I would apply the teachings and hope for the best. The results were amazing. As it turned out, this experience was part of Neshea's teachings. To experience peace and love, we do not have to sit alone in silence. Each life experience offers an opportunity to become aware of the love and joy present in every moment.

What I have learned through this process and gained from these messages has been life-changing. These teachings and practices can help you change your life, too. I invite you to read the messages with an open mind and practice with a willing heart.

Freedom and happiness await . . .

An Encouraging Message to Me from Neshea

I received this message in the beginning when I needed encouragement and confidence. Although this was a personal message, it could be inspiring for everyone.

When you are ready, we will proceed with a way to acknowledge what is valuable to the world but has been forgotten. You are providing a means to allow the world to remember. Helping in this way ensures the continuity of ancient teachings that serve the world throughout time.

What you have remembered is not complicated, but it challenges you to explore your life's deeper purpose. Your life is meant to serve your highest aspiration. What you desire to achieve is not of this world, yet the world is here to help you achieve your goal. Many have forgotten why they are here. These teachings and practices will ignite the flame that will grow into a burning desire to experience Divine love, peace, and joy while living in this world.

Anyone pursuing this worthy goal is a wayshower and will help others remember their Divine purpose. I am a teacher for those who want freedom now and are willing to lead others to greater freedom and happiness while living in this world.

If you are drawn to these teachings, the spark has been ignited in your soul.

A Message to the Reader
from Neshea

My messages are an answer to your deepest questions regarding your experiences while living in this world:

+ You want to know how you can be free of distress, lack, loneliness, pain, and unfulfillment.

+ You want to know how you can experience pure love and connection.

+ You want your experience in this world to have value.

+ You want a Divine purpose for living.

To achieve what you want, there must be a willingness to walk a path largely ignored by the world. This path requires careful attention to your inner world, the boundaries you have set due to fear, and the limitless possibilities of experiences in every present moment. This internal focus can be uncomfortable and exciting at the same time. You might feel uncomfortable because you have forgotten your inherent freedom to explore all experiences available in every moment. You might feel excited because exploring consciousness reminds you that you are a spiritual being whose purpose is to create.

The messages I share encourage you to see your life experiences as your spiritual path. We begin our journey together in Part I with an understanding of the universal answer to all your problems and concerns. In Part II, we identify and dissolve the difficulties you might have in accepting this answer, especially when the world's answers contradict what you are learning. In Part III, we address relationships specifically because they are your most valuable resource and, simultaneously, a major stumbling block to experiencing freedom and joy. And in Part IV, we explore answers to your questions about common life experiences to help you remain clear in your goal and consistent in your practice.

The messages can be savored and enjoyed in any way that feels right. This decision is your first practice in listening to your own inner wisdom and following your own heart. I am here to guide, encourage, and support you along the way. In the end, you will realize that it has always been YOU leading the way. Until then, I will be a symbol of your wisdom and strength.

Your loving Guide,

Neshea

PART I

The Universal Answer

A universal theology is impossible, but a universal experience is not only possible but necessary.

A COURSE IN MIRACLES

February 5

"What would you share with us now?"

Love, adoration, impact, helpfulness—these words signify what we are going to do together. It is important that you realize the impact this has on others. It is helpful for you to know that others will benefit from what you hear. Helpfulness comes in many forms. Love is why you listen and share.

I am here to help you understand, know, and trust your life's purpose. Listen to my words. Write them down. Honor and trust that your intentions are pure.

Love is the answer that we seek. But, to know love, we must first know ourselves. Your helpfulness to the world is to be truthful to who you are and what you came here for. I will never lead you astray, for I love the world as you do. I give you my words as a way to understand ancient teachings that have been forgotten. Trust in what you hear; know it is coming from a pure place. Understand your heart, and you will learn how to be helpful.

These teachings allow you to be present and honor everyone's path as a way to know yourself truly. Love is the guiding light in all things, in all people, in all teachings, and in all life. Hear my words. Listen to the messages and learn how to be free.

"Thank you."

February 6

"What teachings would you share with us now?"

You will know what the answer is when you have the knowledge of your oneness with the Creator and with all creation. All your problems result from not understanding your part of the whole. I am a part of your mind that lives and breathes in the trees, the heavens, the earth—the universe. You are a part of me as I am a part of you. There is nothing more you need to know than this, yet you struggle with the sense of separation from the whole. Unity is the way to be free.

I want to teach you about yourself. Here is how we will go about it:

You first must recognize the problem as it really is. You think you know yourself, but you do not. You love the way you know, yet you do not know the way. Recognizing you don't know is the beginning. I'm here to help you understand who you are because you do not know yourself.

What is it about yourself that you DO know? You are a light.

In ancient times, the light was considered the essence of all things. This light helped us see and know the truth. How can you find this light again? If it is the essence of all things, you must look deeper into all things to find this light. What does that mean? It means you must explore the realms of consciousness that hold this light. How do you do that? You take where you are, and you work from there. Where you are is not who you are, but it is your experience of yourself. You must not deny this experience in order to allow it to transform your concept of yourself.

Your experience is made up of three parts: your ability to love, your ability to see, and your ability to feel. You have decided it is something else that makes up your experience. It is THIS decision that gets in your way of change.

The most difficult task before you is to be fully present to the moment you are in. It contains many levels of experiences that influence you. Each level determines an aspect of the experience you are not always aware of, even though awareness IS your greatest gift and ability. How do you become more aware? It is your willingness to see what is there, to transcend, and to make choices and decisions that lead to greater awareness and happiness.

Your decisions currently are made from superficial levels of desires, needs, and wants. These decisions are not always in your best interest, appealing to the part of you that has forgotten it is light. Good choices can only be made from complete awareness of all levels of consciousness. That is why the ability to love, to see, to feel, and to change are important to being free.

"Thank you."

☙

PRESENT MOMENT MANTRA:
My ability to love, to see, to feel, and to change leads me to greater happiness.

MORNING AND BEDTIME MANTRA:
Divine light is the essence of all things. When I look deeper into all things, I see the light.

February 7

I struggle with how to begin. I am torn between moving on to the next teaching or asking for clarification of the teaching from yesterday. I finally decide to ask for an explanation of the previous message.

"Are there any clarifications from yesterday's teaching you would share with us now?"

It is difficult to understand the best option that leads to the greater good when you fear the answer you seek. That is why you need help in seeing what is there for you to see. You are not meant to live alone in your mind. You have all the answers, yet you don't know how to access what you know. The choices you make and the things you do are from this not knowing. You struggle and suffer because you have forgotten where your answers lie. How can you access what you know? You must be willing to live with greater awareness of all aspects of yourself. Your willingness to do just this is how you love yourself in the moment.

Life is here for you to explore all levels of consciousness and to bring forth the highest version of yourself that serves the world. To do that, you must be open to listening and following what the heart knows to be true. This is a step-by-step process where patience is required.

It is extremely challenging to receive this message. I notice the temptation to finish the sentence with my own words. I pause the recorder numerous times to clear my mind before receiving the next channeled word.

"What would you share regarding the challenge I am having to receive these words and the temptation to fill in words of my own?"

It is difficult to review previous teachings because now you think you already know. THIS is the same problem you have in many situations. Your mind is not open to receiving new information when it thinks it knows something of importance. I am trying to bypass this block and accommodate your request because your intention is to know.

When life happens, moments are filled with preconceived notions that are difficult to bypass. This is what you are experiencing now. Your heart is in the right place, yet your mind focuses on a pinprick and believes that is all there is. Yet, it is only one of the levels that influence the present moment. The challenge you have in receiving clarification of the first teaching IS clarification of the first teaching.

Now, let's use this example to understand how to be open to the present moment and all it contains. Your past learning is getting in the way of knowing. Therefore, you must forget that you ever knew anything at all. You find it especially difficult to forget because you feel lost in the forgetting. It is helpful to remember that forgetting leads to knowing and knowing leads to peace.

I see an image of a whiteboard filled with words. I erase every word until the board is empty. I stare at a stark whiteboard and wait patiently for words of wisdom to be written on the board.

"Thank you."

℘

PRESENT MOMENT MANTRA
I erase from my mind all that I think I know.
I am open to new insights that set me free.

MORNING AND BEDTIME MANTRA
Love is the guiding light in all things, in all people,
in all teachings, and in all life.
Love guides me to become aware of all that is
present in every moment.

February 8

"What would you share with us today that will lead us toward greater happiness?"

Patience is the path to loving yourself. When you agree to be open to communication from me, you open the doorway to seeing yourself from all points of view. Developing your ability to acknowledge and accept yourself enhances your capacity to know yourself.

For instance, when you feel upset and lost, you judge yourself and the moment you are in. This judgment leads to distress, which leads to unhappiness. In contrast, you can allow the experience to teach you everything about the present moment. You will notice both "good" and "bad" traits. Nothing is "good" or "bad," as you have judged it. All things are helpful if you deem them so. Nothing defines you, yet everything teaches you.

You ask how you can find greater happiness while living in the world. Your happiness is already an experience you are having, yet you focus on that pinprick and miss the glory of the moment you are in. You seek happiness by moving chess pieces around the board, believing that one square is better than the other. Yet, each square contains all that you need to experience joy. Until you can rest awhile on a square with patience and understanding, happiness will continue to elude you. I know that this is difficult when parts of the moment contain pain.

Your ability to experience all realms of consciousness at the same time allows you to see, love, and feel beyond your wildest imagination. This expansion does not negate one level of consciousness or replace it with another. It holds all levels simultaneously, allowing you to know yourself better.

Your freedom to decide what you will become aware of determines the degree of happiness you experience. What aspects of your experience you reject or deny become the parts of you that you do not know. If knowing is joy, then you are denying yourself joy. Your willingness to fully experience the present moment is all that is required to reject this denial.

"Thank you."

ᘓ

PRESENT MOMENT MANTRA
Patience is the way to loving myself. I am willing to experience this present moment fully.

MORNING AND BEDTIME MANTRA
Nothing defines me, yet everything teaches me. I am open to perceiving myself from a Divine point of view.

February 9

During my morning meditation, I question the relevance and helpfulness of these teachings. I think of people struggling with illness, unemployment, and loneliness. I wonder how these teachings will benefit them. I then recall my dream where I met Neshea. I remember observing other students enjoying his company, yet I am the only one who asks to interview him. I am hoping today's teachings address these thoughts. I finish my meditation and pick up my recorder. I am ready to receive the next set of words.

You need to be ready for the next learning. Everyone is trying to learn what they already know, yet not everyone is ready to know everything. Your desire is your guide to what you are ready for. If you find yourself drawn to something, it is because you are ready for it. If you are feeling resistance or fear in learning something new, it is only because you have forgotten that you want it. The way to overcome this resistance is to focus on what you desire. When you focus on your desire, your heart feels excited.

You desire insights that allow you to be fully present to everyone and everything in a loving, peaceful way. Through your presence, love, joy, and peace enter the hearts of those you are with and go far beyond where you are. Your presence can heal the world.

Your learning is one of remembering who you are in every moment. I will teach you what you want to know because you are ready to know. Notice how your heart feels right now when you hear these words.

My eyes fill with tears. Simultaneously, my heart feels warm and flutters with excitement.

THIS experience is how you know you are where you want to be.

I will lead you because I love you and hear your call for help in knowing how to be free. When you wonder who will benefit, you have forgotten that the gift is for you. Accept what is offered and know and trust that you cannot receive for yourself alone.

"Thank you."

&

PRESENT MOMENT MANTRA
When I focus on my heart's desire,
I know what is best for me.

MORNING AND BEDTIME MANTRA
I desire insights and guidance that allow me to be fully present
to everyone and everything in a loving, peaceful way.

February 11

"What is important for us to understand about freedom?"

Freedom comes with a price. You look for freedom from conditions that can help you know yourself. These conditions are the best environment for you at the time because it is where you are. You resist this idea because your awareness of your condition and the environment seems to increase the discomfort. When you resist the situation, event, or circumstance, you fail to realize the gift offered in every present moment.

Let us define what freedom is.

You are always free. I said that freedom comes with a price. It is at the cost of realizing you can never be bound by anything you experience. Your realization of your power in any given moment is at the cost of letting go of a weak self-concept. You are a glorious being with great strength, power, and wisdom. The conditions help you learn this truth about yourself. When you tap into your greatest resource, the ability to know yourself, you will realize you have always been free.

"I feel some resistance to this message. What would you share to help me stay open to new learning?"

You want freedom another way. You desire freedom from limitation and still want to continue to limit your self-concept. Once you accept that freedom is expansion, you are ready to learn how to be free. Expansion and freedom are directly linked. Therefore, if you are seeking freedom, it is important to explore what we mean by expansion and how to expand in a world that seems to limit you.

I said before that your ability to love, see, and feel makes up your experience. I used the word "ability" on purpose. If one has an ability, they have the means and resources to achieve what they desire. Yet, the ability does not necessarily indicate mastery. One must practice to gain mastery. Your ability to stretch beyond the boundaries you have set is something you always possess. The restrictions you place around your love, your perceptions, and your feelings, you put in place for protection. From what? You can't remember, yet you still believe you need protection. You are afraid, but you don't know what you are scared of.

There is no enemy beyond the boundaries you have set in place. Learning beyond what you currently know for what you want to remember is a decision YOU must make. This decision can only be made by you. You are in charge of the first step. The rest is given, yet the first step must come from you. That is why expansion is difficult for you. To convince yourself that you want to expand beyond your limited perceptions and feelings when you are unsure you do is challenging. Be gentle. Be patient. Know that you are doing your best and everything you have ever wanted will come to you in due time.

A way to practice gentleness and patience is to ask yourself, "What can I allow into my awareness now?" What you become aware of can be pleasurable or painful. Do not judge. Be happy that you are becoming aware. Awareness is how you practice expansion. It WILL lead to greater happiness and freedom in your life.

"Thank you."

ↁ

PRESENT MOMENT MANTRA
All that I need to experience joy is in this present moment.

MORNING AND BEDTIME MANTRA
I am a glorious being with great strength, power, and wisdom.
There is nothing to fear in expansion.
What can I allow into my awareness now?

February 12

"When we are upset, fearful, uncomfortable, or in physical pain, what can we do to resolve it?"

In your quest to be free, you are remembering your rights as a child of God. You know you are worthy of love, joy, peace, and complete freedom from pain. You need to honor your desire to be free, for it is the remembrance of who you really are. Many try to deny their suffering. Others believe that suffering is part of a Divine plan. And some hold on to suffering because they have forgotten they are worthy of joy. You are a being of light and deserve to be free from all forms of suffering. When one finally decides to be free of pain, they are open to receiving a way to freedom.

Love honors all ways toward freedom. However, there are ways to help you find freedom faster. My way is not the only way. It is important to love everyone's way because this acceptance of others is how you love yourself even when you struggle to find your way. When one holds space for another and honors their way toward freedom, they learn to trust their own way.

In an instant, you can be free from anything that disturbs your peace. Yet, the instant contains many choices that determine how long the moment lasts.

CHOICE #1: Leave the present moment or stay in the moment long enough to transform it.

You are stronger than you realize. You can hold many experiences simultaneously without it affecting your Self at all. Without this perspective, it seems impossible to stand still in a painful present moment. That is why you must commit to doing so, trusting that the truth of who you are prevails in all circumstances and experiences. Your willingness to commit to this choice is part of your strength. Therefore, it is an aspect of your Self shining through in the moment.

CHOICE #2: Judge yourself or love yourself.

You are worthy of adoration and praise for your commitment to exploring the present moment and discovering the essence of your being, which is joy. When the present moment is painful, it is not a time to forget how amazing you are. You are leading yourself to freedom. When you choose to be fully present in the experience you are having, you are not failing. You are succeeding.

CHOICE #3: Take matters into your own hands or allow a change of heart and mind.

Love leads you to right-action. Fear leads you nowhere. The choice to allow a change of heart and mind is essential if you want to experience true freedom and right-action. Once this choice is firmly made, you can trust all the guidance you receive.

CHOICE #4: Deny love or allow feelings of love to enter into your awareness.

This love originates from deep within your being. It is your choice to feel it or not. You can make this choice regardless of your current experience.

You might notice the temptation to deny the love that is there but not yet known. This temptation IS the reason why your commitment to be free from suffering is essential to being free. When you remember that you deserve to be free from pain, you create an opening for love to enter your awareness.

When you make these choices during moments of upset, you neither deny nor reject any aspect of yourself. At the same time, you remain open to expanding your limited understanding. Through acceptance and desire, you have found freedom.

"What would you share regarding our tendency to avoid pain through spiritual means?"

Your question is a judgment. It would be better to ask, "What can you do to avoid delays when you seek freedom from pain?"

You are looking for the easy way but are mistaken in identifying what is easy versus what is hard. Hard is when you reject what will bring release. Easy is when you embrace every part of your experience. Hard is when you insist on going it alone. Easy is when you recognize you are not alone. You avoid delays in finding freedom from pain when you honor everything as a means to know yourself.

Honoring everything means fully experiencing all your feelings, whether sad or happy. You are sometimes more comfortable with feeling angst than you are with feeling joy. Neither one is conditional. They can occur regardless of events or situations that are happening in your world. All feelings are available to you as a light being. WHAT you choose to feel is not as important to your learning as recognizing that YOU are the one who is choosing. Remember, who you are is beyond all experiences, yet all experiences are teaching you. What do I mean when I say that?

Your value is predetermined. No choice you make can change who you are. However, some choices can lead you to greater happiness while you think you live in the world. If you choose joy, feel the joy fully. If you choose sadness, allow yourself to experience it fully. Otherwise, you will forget that you made the choice. Once you fully feel your choice, you are free to choose again.

Life becomes a joyful adventure when you are aware of who you are, regardless of the experience.

"Thank you."

᷍

PRESENT MOMENT MANTRA
It is safe for me to experience this moment fully.
I am a being of pure light.

MORNING AND BEDTIME MANTRA
I am worthy of love, joy, peace, and complete freedom from pain.
I honor my desire to be free, for it is the remembrance of who I am.
I honor all choices that lead to freedom.

February 13

I can't think of a question to ask. I worry that I won't receive a message today if I don't ask a question. Minutes pass as I try to come up with a question. I decide to stop struggling and just be honest.

"No question comes to mind, yet I feel there is more to learn."

For your mind to become aware of all levels of consciousness, you must be open to receiving new information—which means you must be willing to let go of what you already know. Asking questions is a way to be open to receiving something new. This learning step is helpful because a mind that thinks it knows is closed. A COMPLETELY open mind, however, has not yet decided WHAT it needs to know.

You are ready to embark on a journey into the unknown when you don't know what question to ask. This uncertainty means you have not already decided what you want to learn. This open condition necessary for expansive awareness is extremely difficult because the unknown is scary. Remember the pinprick analogy of your mind closing in on a thought, a feeling, or a perception? It can also close in on a question you want the answer to. Deciding what question to ask can be a way to control the outcome and thereby manage your fear. This hidden purpose is not always the reason why you ask a question. Yet, I advise you to be aware if you are using questions to lessen your fear of the unknown.

When you struggle to ask the right question, recognize the value of this confusion. Although questions can be helpful to begin to open your mind, you have reached a new level of learning when you do not know what question to ask. Rejoice in where you are on the journey. Not predicting what answers you'll receive, you are open to knowing everything. This knowing is remembering. If I am you and you are me, then what I tell you is what you tell yourself. You can never be far from knowing everything because you can never be apart from yourself.

How is this information helpful? It highlights the subtle tricks the mind can play and helps you enjoy the ingenuity of the creative mind. At the same time, it creates an environment in which you can be open to receiving the highest, most expansive, and complete awareness of consciousness you are ready for. In this open state, what you receive teaches you there is nothing to fear in knowing yourself. This irrational fear dissipates when you are willing to see IF there is something to fear in expansion. Therefore, when your mind is blank, and you have no question to ask, yet you are open to becoming aware of all that exists in the present moment, rejoice!

∽

PRESENT MOMENT MANTRA
I don't know anything, yet I am willing
to remember everything.
I embrace this state of confusion.
It leads to amazing insights.

MORNING AND BEDTIME MANTRA
I am a being of pure light.
No choice I make affects who I am,
yet every choice can teach me.
The choice I make now is
to embrace every part of the present moment
and let it teach me the truth of who I am.

And, then I receive another message . . .

Now that old learning has been put aside, we will continue to learn something new in the spirit of joy. You will notice the familiarity of what you are learning, yet to understand it, you must be willing to admit you do not know. Paradoxical as that sounds, you need to remain flexible. That is why sometimes it can be helpful to have it appear as if communication is coming from something that is not you when it is YOU who is always leading you. Everything is designed to help you, even the experience of receiving "new" information from an "outside" source.

Be willing to be where you are on the journey. Don't try to skip ahead by pretending you know more than you do. Striving to be spiritually mature is a trick the mind plays to make the game more enjoyable. Maturity is the mastery of your ability to see yourself as you are in any given moment. Love loves you where you are. It does not set conditions for you to meet before love can be experienced. Every moment offers the gift of awareness. Don't try to be somewhere you are not, or you will miss the gift that is offered to you. Every step is the right step because YOU are present in every moment.

"Are all steps internal, or are there times when taking action steps in the world helpful?"

Some steps require you to take action, but for the sole purpose of loving yourself in the moment—especially if you have denied yourself what you need, believing it is for your highest good. If you have misunderstood life as grueling, you must learn that life is meant to be a joyful expression of who you are.

Life is a game that can either be enjoyable or unenjoyable . . .

I interrupt communication because I am troubled by this sentence. We choose whether life is enjoyable, regardless of what is happening? How can we possibly enjoy devastating moments? The message seems insensitive and hurtful to those who have experienced tragedies. For a brief moment, I consider deleting the sentence. Then, it occurs to me that the messages so far have been loving and gentle. Therefore, I might have misunderstood the meaning of the sentence.

"Please clarify the meaning of the last sentence."

Life is not enjoyable when things go well and unenjoyable when things go badly. Life is meant to express light, love, and beauty—the essence of who you are in truth. Tragedies are not enjoyable. They are opportunities to let the expression of Divine truth enter the present moment. When you recognize moments of distress as opportunities for the light to enter and realize YOU are this light, you turn tragedies into expressions of Divine truth. When this occurs through your willingness to make good choices (outlined in a previous message), you learn just how enjoyable life can be.

Do not mistake unhappiness for joy. Unhappiness is unhappiness, and joy is joy. Do not be content with unhappiness. Do not love unhappiness. Do not see unhappiness as spiritual. But rather, recognize unhappiness as a vehicle to joy and do your best to practice these teachings. That is the way you embrace everything and at the same time accept nothing less than pure happiness as your experience while living in this world.

"Thank you."

ↁ

PRESENT MOMENT MANTRA
Love loves me where I am.

MORNING AND BEDTIME MANTRA
*Moments of distress are not failures. They are opportunities
for Divine light to enter.*

February 14

"What teaching would you share with us today?"

Everyone wants to be free of problems. Everyone has the right to be free. The way to find freedom, however, is not always obvious to the one who seeks solutions to their problems.

I find myself looking ahead to see what word comes next before speaking the channeled word into the recorder.

"What will you share to help me stay in the present moment?"

You are having trouble because you want to know what comes next to ensure that it is something you want to hear. You have the same trouble when trying to solve problems in the world. You look ahead to possible answers that will be acceptable to you. What do you know about the nature of your problem, where it originated, or what it is comprised of? Unless you understand all facets that make up the problem, you will avoid finding the solution.

Problems are the main reason you seek answers and can be the catalyst to finding what you are always searching for. When the world offers no solutions to your problems, you are finally on the right track. You do not need to understand the nature of your problem, yet you do need help in finding the solution. Wouldn't it be amazing if you were offered the solution without any effort and from a source that knows exactly what the problem is and how to solve it? That is what is offered to you in every moment. However, it is difficult to get through the defenses you set up. Instead of dissecting the problem, your time would be better spent understanding your defenses to receive the solution.

DEFENSE #1: You want to be in charge of deciding the solution.

You think you know best what will make you happy and feel secure within a world that seems to deny you your happiness. You fear that a solution from a Divine source will deny you what you want and cause more problems.

To lower this defense, remind yourself that heaven is meant to be experienced on earth. All solutions offered to you from Divine wisdom lead to joy.

A simple question will suffice to lower this defense. Ask Divine wisdom, "What solution will work to solve the problem?"

DEFENSE #2: You insist on dissecting the problem and the solutions available to you.

This analytical approach to problem-solving limits your understanding of the problem and the solutions you will accept. You believe that in understanding the problem, the answer will make sense to you. Yet, your understanding couldn't possibly encompass the whole problem. Therefore, to accept a Divine solution, you must let go of the need to understand the nature of your problem.

You possess true understanding. When you dissect the problem and the solutions, you forget that there is a part of you that already knows.

There is a much quicker process to access this knowledge. Trust the wisdom you already possess and ask, "What do I need to understand right now?"

DEFENSE #3: You doubt the answers you receive.

Doubting is a defense that leads to chaos. You are confused about who you are when you doubt what you know from the deep reservoir of knowledge that is your birthright. Doubting is viewed as healthy skepticism. Actually, it is used as a defense to becoming aware of the whole, which cuts you off from the solution.

When you release Defense #1 and Defense #2, you begin to know what will solve the real problem. Engaging in Defense #3 is your last defense to receiving what you want. When you doubt what you know, you return to Defense #1 and start the cycle again.

To lower Defense #3, trust the Divine answers you receive. Trust means following through. Only then will you know that the solution you were given was the answer.

I am being vague regarding specific solutions for a reason. You want a set of solutions to be spelled out for every problem you have. This would not be helpful nor honoring everyone's individual path to freedom. Love finds a way to be helpful in all circumstances. It will offer the best solution within the perimeters you have set. As you grow in your readiness to expand your understanding of the real problem and the ultimate truth that sets you free from all problems, love's answers grow with you.

Pushing yourself to receive what you are not ready for is unloving to yourself. Continue to strive to be ready to receive the ultimate truth and, at the same time, remain open to the way love is answering you now.

"Thank you."

❧

PRESENT MOMENT MANTRA
Divine wisdom understands the nature of my problem and the answer that will set me free.

MORNING AND BEDTIME MANTRA
Love finds a way to be helpful in all circumstances. I remain open to the way Divine love is answering me now.

February 15

I feel discouraged this morning as I prepare to receive a message. I question again whether these teachings are helpful to those who are struggling. I want the instructions to serve others who are in pain. I want . . . my thoughts are interrupted by these channeled words:

Walk your path. Others might or might not follow.

Your struggles have served you well. You have met each one with a desire to authentically search for a way that works to free you from the struggle. The desire for freedom requires you to be fully present in all your experiences.

I feel resistance to receiving the next channeled words.

You are finding it difficult to listen to me now because you fear you did not do it right. There is no "right" or "wrong" way. However, there are ways that work, ones that do not, and those that take more time. I am teaching a way that seems difficult because it requires complete honesty and a willingness to feel uncomfortable. Your way to be free is not one that everyone chooses. All is well whether one chooses a way or not.

To truly love one another means accepting everyone's choices knowing everyone will receive what they desire. Releasing others with confidence that they know their own heart frees you to follow your way. To love is not to judge. To love is to acknowledge everyone's right to be free and to remind them that they deserve to experience happiness, peace, and love.

"Thank you. I am ready to listen now."

Following your heart's desire and what YOU are ready for is a way to be helpful. All levels of learning teach you something of value. What I want to teach you will save you time. Time is for you to use constructively in a manner that helps you reach a heavenly state of mind. All you need to do is trust your way. Don't worry about how your choice affects others. Your love for the world will ensure that your way blesses the world.

Now, let us consider the goal of a heavenly state of mind.

This goal is not appealing to everyone, yet to reach this goal is to use the world constructively. "Heaven is a state of mind" is a truth with practical meaning. It means you are present in every moment in such a way that blesses the world with what it needs at the time. The world does not always recognize its greatest need. Those who seek this goal understand the world, its needs, and its purpose.

Do you want a heavenly state of mind? The answer would be "yes" if you knew its value. Keep its value close to your heart, especially in times of struggle. Knowing its value will keep you on track toward freedom and true helpfulness. If you forget its preciousness to you, you will pursue other goals that are not as helpful as a heavenly state of mind can be.

It is not selfish to pursue what is valuable to you when others struggle because your state of mind is important to the well-being of others. I have described this state of mind in the first few messages. You can return to these messages whenever you waver in recognizing the value of this goal. The messages remind you of what you seek to improve your life and the lives of others. When you focus on what OTHERS can do to influence their situation, you forget how YOU can influence the whole.

Let's take a moment to remember the way you can be truly helpful. You are the light the situation needs. Recognizing what is needed, you turn your attention inward and focus on the choices YOU can make. Your peace is what the situation requires. Authentic peace comes with the awareness of all levels of consciousness—the real and the unreal, the true and the false—within one's present moment. Once you have firmly established the value of this heavenly state of mind, you will naturally be open to ways to reach this goal.

"Thank you."

&

PRESENT MOMENT MANTRA
To love is not to judge myself or others.
To love is to honor everyone's right to be free.

MORNING AND BEDTIME MANTRA
My state of mind is important to the well-being of others.
I turn my attention inward and focus on the choices
I can make that lead to a heavenly state of mind.

February 16

"Today, I feel anticipation and excitement. I am beginning to enjoy the experience of not knowing what message I will receive. It's fun to be surprised."

The unexpected can be exhilarating if you allow the experience to teach you who you are. Unfortunately, most use the occasion to try to return to the familiar, believing that what is familiar is a desired outcome. All your efforts to provide safety and comfort are a way to love yourself in the moment. Yet, you fail to realize that these gifts to yourself are based upon a belief that you must experience limitations to feel safe.

You only know a small portion of the answers that will remind you that you are cared for and loved. The answers that arise from your limited awareness can provide some comfort at the moment, yet they can keep you trapped within a narrow version of yourself and reality. When you allow an expanded perception of your reality, you are open to unexpected answers that have the potential to free you from the burden of always trying to feel safe.

You are always safe. Yet, in this world, you forget this fact, not because the world is unsafe, but because you limit your awareness. Understandably, you seek answers that appear to provide safety and comfort when you do not see your reality as it is in truth. If you can allow yourself to enjoy the unexpected, to be surprised rather than wanting the next moment to be familiar, you will remain open to receiving new answers. Not only will the answers provide safety and comfort—they will teach you the truth about who you are.

The moment before you know what comes next is a precious moment. When it is experienced as fearful, you tend to anticipate all possible outcomes. You are trying to prepare for the next moment by grasping onto something familiar. This reaction repeats the cycle of limitation and narrows your awareness, which defeats the purpose of opening to the unexpected.

To break this cycle, first, recognize that your need to know what comes next is based on your fear of the unknown. Next, when you are afraid, love yourself more, not less. A restful mind, in a state of anticipation, hears the voice of Divine wisdom. Trust in this wisdom, not in your ability to figure things out. When you take a step, pause, and be willing to be surprised at what comes next.

"Is every step always peaceful?"

Every step LEADS to peace. Peace is the awareness that you are always safe and cared for in every moment. When you step into the unfamiliar, however, you might feel uncomfortable. This discomfort is a sign of expansion.

Let us be clear that not all steps are action steps in the world. Steps can be inward movements toward new beliefs, self-concepts, or feelings. With each step, you leave behind something as you gain something else. All steps, when taken in a heartfelt manner, require gentleness and patience. When you can embrace and love feeling uncomfortable, you will know you are ready to take the next step. If you are terrified, you are not ready.

Becoming ready does not require time. It requires a willingness to embrace everything happening in the present moment. You cannot skip ahead, although it might seem there are steps that you can skip. When you try to avoid an unpleasant moment by skipping ahead, you will find the same substance of thought, feeling, and perception in the next present moment, even though your surroundings have changed. Do not be upset to learn that

PART I: The Universal Answer – February 16

this idea is true. It is a joyful realization that no matter your choice, you are always on the right step. When you can love this fact, peace will be yours.

"Thank you."

෫

PRESENT MOMENT MANTRA
No matter what choice I make,
I am in the right place and on the right step
to experience love, peace, and joy.

MORNING AND BEDTIME MANTRA
When I know I am safe, life is a joyful adventure.
I am open to unexpected answers that teach me I am safe
and cared for in every moment.

February 18

"I do not know what message I am ready to receive next. I am willing to trust that whatever it is, the message will be what I want."

I feel anxious and uncomfortable as I wait to receive the channeled words.

The moment you release the idea that you know what you want, there is a concern that you will not have what you need. You always know the truest desire of your heart. Yet, you believe that to get what you want, you must travel through difficulties and struggles to receive it. Therefore, what you want is not freedom but difficulties.

I am teaching you a way that avoids difficulties in getting what you want. This way seems challenging because it is easy. Easy is not a way you are familiar with, although it is a way that is available to you. You must choose the way. You will choose the hard way if you believe that struggling leads to greater accomplishments.

I am finding it difficult to receive the words that come next. I am fully aware that I am doing exactly what the message just highlighted. I am making this process harder than it needs to be.

"What can you share that will help me choose the easy way?"

The easy way requires surrender. You are not in charge of the easy way. You would rather be in charge of how you find freedom, even if your way is difficult. You believe that relinquishing control means you are sacrificing what you want. Yet, it is you trying to take control that is interfering with the flow. If you want control, you have chosen a difficult way.

The resistance to releasing control of deciding what you want, is strong. It is based on the fear that if you surrender to the easy way, you will not have what you need. The easy way is to let Divine wisdom lead the way. If you choose the easy way but then look ahead and conclude that where you are headed is not where you want to go, you will take charge again. This moment can be a teachable moment if you are willing to recognize WHY this has occurred.

You fear that nothing will happen if you stop making things happen through sheer determination to steer your life in a certain direction. Ultimately, you fear there is no flow—no Divine energy moving you to where you want to go, how you want to feel, and what you want to experience. You must believe there is no Divine flow if you think that letting go of controlling your direction means nothing will happen. Yet in this precise moment, when you release control, the Divine energy of all creation can flow through your experience to give you everything you want.

You are finding it easier to receive my words now, which means you are learning the easy way.

"It is easier now for me to receive your words. Why do I continue to feel uncomfortable?"

Your feelings of discomfort can be attributed to being in unfamiliar territory where you are not in charge. Love the experience of feeling uncomfortable, and you will resist the temptation to take control. When you do not know what comes next and you are willing to follow directions, you are choosing the easy way.

A simple practice to surrender control and choose the easy way is to get in the habit of asking, "What comes next?" Be prepared to receive a word, a feeling, a perception, or an action. All are in the realm of guidance from a higher source who knows what you want. Do not judge what you receive. If there is a question about whether it is part of the easy way, you can ask for clarification and validation. Restate that you do not know what is best for you right now. You DO know that you want the easy way, and if what you have received puts you on the difficult path, you do not want it. Now, you are willing to be led. This response is how you ensure your happiness as you practice choosing the easy way.

I entertain the possibility that I have interjected my thoughts into the writings and, therefore, tainted the messages. This thought puts me in a melancholy mood.

You are learning that when you are in charge, you are choosing the difficult way. When Divine wisdom guides you in all things, you are choosing your happiness. See this feeling of sadness as progress toward getting what it is you want. When you recognize that what you want is the easy way, and it is yours when you let go of being in charge, you surrender more readily and willingly to what comes next.

Today, practice not being in charge. Allow yourself to be surprised by an unexpected thought, feeling, perception, or action. The experience will teach you that the easy way is not difficult.

"How can I discern between random thoughts, ideas, and actions generated by overthinking and thoughts, ideas, and actions originating from Divine wisdom?"

Everything leads to freedom in the end. Some thoughts, ideas, and actions make life more difficult if you choose to follow them. The difficulties can lead you to a greater awareness of what you want, which is the easy way. Following thoughts, ideas, and actions to their natural conclusion is okay. If they lead to peace and a gentle, loving experience, you know they originated from the highest wisdom you were ready for. If they lead to strife, simply choose again, knowing that this awareness has led you to choose the easy way.

As you become clearer that the easy way is the one you want—thoughts, ideas, and actions will naturally align with your choice. Eventually, when you are 100% certain you want the easy way 100% of the time, you will not have to question the source of your thoughts, ideas, and actions.

Never judge your choices. Instead, use each choice as an opportunity to teach you that you deserve the easy way.

"Thank you."

☙

PRESENT MOMENT MANTRA
*I want the easy way. I am open to
thoughts, feelings, perceptions, and actions
that align with what I want.*

MORNING AND BEDTIME MANTRA
*When I let Divine wisdom guide me in all things,
I am choosing my happiness. I release control and
let the Divine energy of all creation flow through
my experience, giving me everything I want.*

February 19

"I am ready to begin."

I want to begin this morning with a message that will clear up any misunderstandings you might have that prevent you from opening your mind to all possibilities that exist in the present moment.

These possibilities encompass all levels of consciousness and remain available to you for your pleasure. Love is the reason they exist as possibilities for you to experience. Your willingness to experience the ultimate level of consciousness, which is the true essence of your Divine nature and the oneness of all creation, grows exponentially when you recognize the freedom you inherently have to examine each level.

The barrier you believe exists between the levels does not exist. You can easily pass through this imagined barrier. Instead, you conceive that it holds you within a level of experience because you want to continue to experience that level. These levels contain varying degrees of love, feelings, and perceptions. What you call the "lower level" is a diminished experience of the "highest level." It's as if you water down the understanding of the ultimate truth to continue to experience this lower level.

When you are only aware of one level at a time, it seems as if other levels do not exist. This limited view helps you maintain your version of reality, which is your chosen experience at the time. Your willingness to pass through the imagined barriers depends on whether or not you desire to experience greater love, deeper feelings, and a more expansive perception of who you are. In practical terms, this means you seek a better understanding of the present moment. You do not cling to your ideas and are willing to feel something different.

If you feel fear, you are willing to feel love. If you feel sadness, you are willing to feel joy. If you feel guilt, you are willing to feel innocence. If you feel anger, you are willing to feel peace.

It is impossible to feel differently while holding on to your understanding. Many have tried to retain their judgments and failed to feel differently, and this failure has caused hopelessness. Remember, as a child of God, you can enjoy ALL experiences and feelings available within the realm of all levels of consciousness. The real reason you do not experience a change of heart is that you have been unwilling to change your mind. This unwillingness creates an imagined barrier that holds you within that experience.

I tell you these things to restore hope and to remind you of your power in every circumstance. Please remember that all helpful teachings are meant to guide you through the maze of your created world. You are never without Divine help to find your way into another experience that would be a more joyful expression of who you are.

Now, I would like to speak to you about the tendency to want to escape rather than expand. The need to escape is rooted in the belief that you are trapped by a power outside your will. This belief creates an urge to break free from opposing forces. These forces can be perceived as external or internal. One might believe they are trapped within an experience by an opposing society that wants to hold them down. One might believe they are trapped by their own mind that has power over what they think, feel, and perceive. This belief creates an intense need to escape to be free.

It is of utmost importance that you do not judge yourself. It does not matter if you believe the barrier that prevents you from experiencing freedom is self-imposed or externally placed there. The idea that a barrier exists at all is what you need to escape from. Luckily, you can escape from ideas easily because they are merely ideas, not facts.

Allow yourself to entertain the idea that your desire to experience something else, your willingness to release your understanding, and your decision to no longer experience your current state is all you need to change your experience. Suddenly, the barriers that seem to hold you back disappear. Now, you can expand to a new feeling, a new thought, and a new perception. The intensity of love increases as your awareness expands.

I recall moments in the past when I had a desire and a willingness to experience something different, yet I continued to feel tethered to my current experience.

"What would help us when we have done what you suggested, yet we still feel something is holding us back?"

Whatever is holding you back needs to be addressed. Otherwise, you are fighting yourself. What holds you back or tethers you to your current experience can appear external, yet I assure you that your external conditions could not possibly have more power over you than your own heart and mind.

Always begin with love. Love your awareness that you desire to expand and that you feel tethered. Love your willingness to find release. Love your courage and strength that has brought you to this moment of awareness. Then, look lovingly at what holds you back from experiencing the desired change. Most likely, you are afraid of what you desire for reasons that you must uncover. A simple inquiry will suffice to aid in this discovery.

Consider the change you desire and ask yourself:

+ What am I afraid of?
+ What do I believe will happen?
+ What do I think I will lose?

Once these questions are answered, do not believe the answers. Instead, question their validity by asking:

+ Is all of it true?

+ Is none of it true?

+ Is some of it true?

Then listen to your deepest knowing.

"Thank you."

ↂ

PRESENT MOMENT MANTRA
I honor all experiences and, at the same time,
remember I am always free to choose a new
thought, feeling, and perception.

MORNING AND BEDTIME MANTRA
I love my awareness. I love my willingness.
I love my strength and courage. I love my ability
to listen to my deepest knowing.

February 20

I turn the recorder on. I notice how comfortable I am with not knowing what message will come through today. The experience of the unknown is much more enjoyable when I surrender in complete trust.

"I am ready to listen. What would you share with us today?"

Today's teachings will bring you great joy. They will answer your deepest questions about why you are not always joyful.

Life is a merry-go-round. You remain seated, securely rooted, and safe to experience the ride. The scenery changes while you remain securely fastened to your seat. Sometimes, the scenery changes slowly. Other times it spins so fast that it can be difficult to make out what you see. Regardless of how fast or slow your environment changes, YOU have not changed. You remain seated, where you can enjoy the ride without falling.

What makes the ride enjoyable is knowing where you are regardless of how fast or slow the ride spins around. You believe that joy comes from the scenery, and when the scenery changes, you lose your joy. To think of life as a merry-go-round will help you remember that what makes life enjoyable is realizing it is a ride.

The thrill of a ride results from the unexpected twists and turns, ups and downs, and changes in the scenery. The ride would not be enjoyable if you lost sight of where you are and how securely you are fastened to your seat. Without this realization, you would try to control the ride by minimizing its ups and downs, predicting its twists and turns, and keeping the scenery stationery so you don't feel like you will fall off the ride. Now, the ride becomes work, and you are exhausted trying to keep yourself safe. If you suddenly realized that you were completely safe and secure, you would put your hands in the air and enjoy the thrill of the ride. Therefore, this message will focus on how to realize where you are and how safe you are so you can enjoy the ride.

Think of how a baby must feel when securely held and carried by a loving parent. A baby knows it cannot walk yet and does not understand how to get to where it needs to go. Realizing their limitations, the baby relaxes and allows themselves to be carried. Life can be like that for you if you recognize that you are being safely carried through life.

The realization that you are securely fastened within your seat and that you are being safely carried through life are awarenesses you must gain to make life enjoyable. These realizations will bring you great joy and a sense of freedom beyond what the world offers to you, with promises of freedom and joy.

You might be thinking that this teaching is not very enjoyable. Maybe you were hoping for a way to find your joy from things in the world. It is okay to enjoy the world, but it is not your source of joy. And, in fact, until you discover real joy, you will not be able to enjoy the world because you will not feel safe on the ride.

"It seems difficult to turn away from the world as a source of happiness and instead desire these realizations. What would you share to help us turn in the right direction to find real joy?"

To be in the world but not of the world is the ultimate freedom. To enjoy the world without it being your source of happiness is a joyful experience. It is helpful to realize that when you seek happiness from things in the world, you are looking to feel safe. Until you feel safe, you cannot enjoy the world. Once you feel safe, your life becomes an enjoyable adventure.

"I never considered safety to be a part of joy. Can you speak more about this teaching?"

Joy is an emotion. Safety is a fact of what you are. "You are safe" is a fundamental aspect of your nature. When you recognize this fact, you naturally feel joyful. You are then free to enjoy the ride you call life.

"Can you help us understand this message in practical terms?"

When you are not joyful, ask yourself, "Do I know I am safe, loved, and cared for?" If you do not know this to be absolutely true, pray for the awareness that it IS true. Your answer might appear as a thought, a sense, or a perception. The answer might be given through someone else or something in the world. Keep an open mind, and do not judge how the answer comes to you. If you have learned that you are safe, cared for, and loved, then it is the perfect answer for you. Now, watch how naturally joy arises and how free you feel to enjoy the ride.

Practice this way regardless of the ride's ups and downs and twists and turns to help you discover the source of joy in every moment.

"I am not enjoying this message. What would you share to help me release resistance and embrace this teaching?"

You are mishearing what I am saying if you resist hearing this message. The world is meant to be enjoyed, yet it is not the source of your joy. If it were, you would be unhappy indeed. This message directs you to experience consistent joy. Why would you not want to be happy all of the time? If you consider that my message helps you find happiness and security within a world that offers neither, you will begin to enjoy today's message. Your life can then become an enjoyable ride.

I want to share a second part of this message with you now.

We often forget about tenderness as part of our awakening to the awareness of all levels of consciousness. "Tenderness" is a word that is not often used, yet it can be helpful when you struggle with teachings that can be misunderstood as leading you away from joy. The word conjures up feelings of warmth and comfort, which can be especially helpful when one feels they are being asked to sacrifice. Just saying the word helps you feel comforted.

I pause to repeat the word over and over again in my mind. I do feel comforted!

I offer these teachings with the utmost tenderness and care for your well-being. Sometimes gifts at first glance do not appear to be gifts. If you believe you are being offered something that is not what you want, it can be helpful to remind yourself that it is offered with tenderness and love, and the giver wants you to be happy and free. Although you might still be hesitant to take the gift, when you are aware of the energy surrounding it, you will trust that it is something you want and will be open to receiving it.

"Thank you."

✑

PRESENT MOMENT MANTRA

The source of joy is the awareness that I am safe, loved, and cared for at this moment.

MORNING AND BEDTIME MANTRA
Divine wisdom wants me to be happy and free. I relax and let myself be safely and lovingly carried through this moment.

February 21

During my morning meditation, I ponder the importance of investigating unconscious beliefs. It is the first time I have noticed an interest in examining the content of the levels of consciousness. I wonder if this curiosity is a distraction or an indication that I am ready for this teaching.

"I acknowledge my curiosity and, at the same time, accept that the content of the levels might not be the message you would share today."

Good morning. Your curiosity leads you to what you are ready to know. Pay attention to what interests you because it is your Self leading you on the journey. Be curious yet remain flexible. Do not cling to any teaching or understanding. Be open about how it can serve you best, yet be willing to move toward what comes next. In this way, you can be sure you are using time efficiently and miraculously.

One caveat to be aware of is your love of learning. Wanting always to learn yet not to know keeps you on a treadmill where it appears that you are moving, yet you are not. Learning leads to knowledge. When you know all you need to know from a teaching or a practice, be ready to move on to what comes next. This flexibility ensures a smooth and effortless journey. Now, let us focus on WHAT you are curious to learn about.

A preoccupation with examining the content of one level of consciousness can delay expanding your awareness to include ALL levels. That does not mean your curiosity about the content of the levels will lead you astray. I only wish to point out some trappings that can occur when you are curious to learn something new. A preoccupation with examining unconscious beliefs can be the same deterrent as a preoccupation with the desire to explore the level of consciousness some call Nirvana.

That is not to say that experiencing the levels is not part of what I am teaching you. Remember, the preoccupation can be the issue, not the experience of one or more levels. When you are curious to examine the content of one of the levels of consciousness, you are open to knowing another aspect of yourself—which is the essence of what I am teaching you. Therefore, it is essential to honor your curiosity.

In any given moment, all levels of consciousness exist at the same time. Where you focus your attention creates your experience of the present moment. Depending on your willingness, you can expand your focus to encompass many levels in one moment of time. For instance, during a moment of your day, you might be aware of feelings, thoughts, physical sensations, or buried thoughts that you call unconscious beliefs. But there is even more to be aware of in that moment.

Are you aware of the pure love that holds all things within itself? Are you aware of the unity and connection of all that exists in the moment? Are you aware of the higher level of thought that understands the true nature of all that is seen and unseen? You see, there is so much more to the present moment than you realize.

For example, when you perceive lack, you might be aware of the feeling of fear. You might also be mindful of the thought that you are lacking and aware of the belief that you are undeserving. You might notice feelings of sadness and guilt. You might also be aware of your desire to be free of the emotions and beliefs about yourself. Isn't it amazing that you can be aware of so many things in one moment? But there is more! You can recall memories of where your self-concept originated and additional memories of this concept being reinforced through life experiences. But there is so much more!

In that moment, there is a memory of your creation, an awareness of your pure innocence, an understanding of how all things work together for good, and the essence of Divine love connecting all things to Itself. When you are aware of all of this—of all that is true and untrue, you can now say that you are fully present in the moment.

Let us now return to your curiosity about the content of the levels of consciousness and why it is important to follow this curiosity. If being fully present in the moment means you are aware of all that exists at that moment, you must not deny, reject, or be afraid of any of the levels. That is why it might be important to examine and correct unconscious beliefs, especially false beliefs about love. You might also need to spend parts of your journey feeling and resolving painful memories and emotions. These are all helpful practices. They can and will lead you to accept and love all levels that exist in the present moment. When you are no longer trying to hold anything apart from your awareness, you are free to expand.

"Thank you."

℘

PRESENT MOMENT MANTRA
*I accept and love all that exists in the present moment—
the seen and the unseen, the true and the false.
This acceptance leads to expansion.*

MORNING AND BEDTIME MANTRA
*I honor all aspects of my journey. I let my curiosity
guide me to the right next step.*

February 22

Normally, I refrain from doing daily tasks and spend time in silence before receiving the message for the day. This morning, my usual routine was interrupted by a phone call. I talked on the phone for thirty minutes and then settled in to receive today's message.

"Now that I have engaged in a daily activity, I am concerned that my mind is too active, and I will not be able to hear the message."

Be ready. Be open. Be willing.

Readiness, openness, and willingness are required to receive what you need at any moment. Preparation to receive what you need in the moment is not required.

You believe you must DO something to receive what you need. A simpler way is to allow whatever you need to be given. Allowing is not the same as doing or preparing. If you feel you must prepare yourself, it would be better for you to do it in this way:

1. Be ready by focusing your attention on the present moment. Let go of the moment that came before the moment you are in. Do not recall the previous moment's content by mulling it over. Let it go, and it is gone.

2. Be open to receiving all that is given in the present moment by not judging what comes next. Do not judge what you need or what is best for you. Releasing judgment creates an opening for you to receive what is being given.

3. Be willing to adjust to what happens next by becoming curious about what is present to you now. Willingness is the flexibility to adapt to something new and unexpected. Your willingness increases as you learn that the unexpected can be amazing. Looking for the gifts in the present moment helps you to be ready, open, and willing more quickly.

These three simple steps not only allow you to receive my words—they are also the catalyst to expanded awareness. There are so many beautiful things to be seen and experienced in the present moment. If you believe you must prepare to receive all that the moment contains, you must also believe that you are not ready. Do you see how this belief can prevent you from having everything you need? The belief that you need to prepare is strong in your mind. That is why I offer you a bridge of three simple steps that eventually will lead you away from this belief.

Now, I want to return to yesterday's message about the content of the levels of consciousness. Some clarification is needed to avoid delays in experiencing the highest level. You think of the highest and lowest levels in terms of up and down. When I speak of the highest level of consciousness, I am referring to the purest love that exists within all levels. Think of it this way: When you ride an elevator, you are only aware of the four walls surrounding you. You are unaware of the shaft that keeps you securely in place, regardless of where the ride takes you. To be aware of the highest level of consciousness, you only need to see through the walls to what is always there.

You have the ability to see through the walls to the shaft of love that holds you and keeps you safe. You need to be ready, open, and willing to use this ability. That is why I suggested you examine the contents of any level you have denied or rejected. This acceptance turns a solid wall into a thin veil you can easily see through.

You will not become preoccupied with examining the levels if you remember that the purpose of examining the content of the levels is to become aware of the love that surrounds you.

"Why do we struggle with this practice?"

You want the walls to show you this love. Yet, it is the walls that hide the love that is there. When the walls fail to show you this love, you mistakenly believe it doesn't exist in the moment you are in. You think that what you need exists in a future moment. That is why you try to move on to the next moment to get what you need and struggle with this practice. You want a practice to learn how to get what you do not have right now. I am teaching you that everything you need is where you are.

This idea is challenging to accept when surrounded by walls that seem to trap you in a painful moment. That is why I gave you these questions to examine the walls more closely: What do you see? What do you feel? What memories do you judge as painful? What do you fear is true about you? (Message given on February 19th.)

When you question the validity of the answers, the walls begin to fade away. Now, you can be aware of the love holding you the whole time.

"Thank you."

&

PRESENT MOMENT MANTRA
Everything I need is right here.
I am ready, open, and willing to receive what I need now.

MORNING AND BEDTIME MANTRA
Love permeates all things.
Let me become aware of the love surrounding me
and keeping me safe.

February 24

"Life is full of both good and bad experiences. We want to hurry through the bad to get to the good. Can you speak more about how we can make EVERY moment count?"

Every moment, whether it be a moment in the past or the present while asleep or awake, offers you information that can help you experience the truth of who you are. This truth is your greatest joy and achievement while living in this world. Every action, thought, feeling, and perception can either show you who you are or what is blocking you from knowing who you are. That is why you can always learn from every experience. That is why nothing is "bad," and all things lead to "good." In contrast, you believe there are both "good" and "bad" experiences.

When you are aware of what blocks you from knowing who you are, you might experience feelings, thoughts, and perceptions that you judge as painful and, therefore, classify as "bad." This reaction can lead you to take action to find relief from what you have judged as "bad." Any remedies that provide temporary relief you judge as "good." These actions generally do not erase the "bad" thoughts, feelings, and perceptions. You then search for other remedies that you believe will eradicate the pain. If they work temporarily, you judge these remedies as "good."

Running in circles will ultimately lead you to question your way out of pain and discomfort, which is good. "Good" in this context means anything that guides you toward greater happiness and fulfillment. If every experience offers you information to guide you toward happiness, then every moment can be judged as "good."

Life is full of teachable moments. Again, these moments, whether in the past, while awake, or asleep, teach you the truth of who you are or what is blocking you from knowing who you are. When you experience peace, freedom, joy, and love for all existence, including yourself, you are using the moment to become aware of the truth of who you are. When you experience pain, fear, unworthiness, powerlessness, hate, and so on, you are using the moment to teach you what is blocking you from knowing who you really are.

It is important to remember this teaching when experiencing uncomfortable feelings, disturbing thoughts, and fearful perceptions. If you mistakenly accept these experiences as the truth of who you are or who others are, you lose sight of the "good" in the present moment. The "good" is the awareness that the experience of pain is teaching you what thoughts, feelings, and perceptions are in the way of you knowing the truth. When you allow the experience to provide helpful information about what prevents you from experiencing joy, fulfillment, and love, you make the most of every moment—including the ones you have judged as "bad."

There are two things I want you to remember to make every moment count:

1. If you feel joy, fulfillment, love, unity, and peace, you are in touch with the truth of who you are. Be happy that this is so.

2. If you feel pain, fear, discomfort, and sadness, you are gaining information that will help you know yourself better. Be happy that this is so.

Once you see the value of what the moment can teach you, you can now make every moment count.

"I am open to any other words of wisdom you would share regarding this topic."

In your quest to be free, you must allow all experiences to aid you in becoming free. Avoiding pain and discomfort prevents you from feeling free because you now believe that an experience can trap you. That is why you avoid it. Evading can be sought through denial, rejection, projection, or running toward the next moment, hoping that what you are trying to avoid does not follow you. True freedom is knowing you can face anything because of your inherent strength as a spiritual being. And because of your unity with the whole, you are never without help to find your way into a new experience.

Also, be aware of your need for others to comply with YOUR wishes. This demand is a subtle way to avoid your internal struggle. When you learn that you offer yourself your freedom, you can allow others to find their own way. If others demand you comply with THEIR wishes, they believe they are trapped in their internal struggle. If both parties believe they are trapped, there will be conflict. If you remember you can use the experience to face the internal struggle and choose to know yourself better; the conflict lessens. When this choice transforms your experience into one of joy, fulfillment, and love, you learn that you offer yourself your freedom. Now, you are free to love regardless of others' choices. Now, you can allow others to choose for themselves without it affecting you.

I am being reminded of the elevator analogy given in a previous message received on February 22nd. I return to the message and reread this paragraph:

"When you ride an elevator, you are only aware of the four walls surrounding you. You are unaware of the shaft that keeps you securely in place, regardless of where the ride takes you. To be aware of the highest level of consciousness, you only need to see through the walls to what is always there. You have the ability to see through the walls to the shaft of love that holds you and keeps you safe."

"*Thank you.*"

൦൦

PRESENT MOMENT MANTRA
This moment is precious because it offers valuable information to help me know myself better.

MORNING AND BEDTIME MANTRA
My greatest joy and achievement is experiencing the truth of who I am. Every moment offers me this gift.

February 25

"When we are upset and unhappy, there can be a strong urge to change jobs, careers, relationships, and locations. How can we discern if the desire to change and manifest something new is in our best interest or if it's avoidance?"

It has been said that wherever you go, there you are, which means you cannot make a wrong choice. However, you can delay your happiness if you believe that all you need is a change of environment to be happy. A change in location, a job, or a relationship, combined with a shift in attitude, beliefs, and purpose, can serve you well. When you believe the ONLY necessary change is external to yourself, a change of environment will not result in permanent happiness.

A change in attitude, beliefs, and purpose is helpful at the beginning of any change. When you are unhappy in the present moment, realize that this experience is helping you become aware of an aspect of yourself. Appreciate all that the present moment is teaching you and acknowledge what is there for you to become mindful of in that moment.

Your beliefs about what is happening, why, and what to do to restore love, happiness, and peace will determine the success or failure of any change you make to your environment. Examine your beliefs closely with honesty and a willingness to recognize what you believe. If these beliefs point to untruths about yourself, such as powerlessness, weakness, vulnerability, guilt, and so on, be willing to change these beliefs to reflect your expanded understanding of the truth of who you are.

For an external change to lead to happiness, the purpose of the change must be for everyone to experience love. "Everyone" includes anyone you leave behind and anyone you will meet. If you struggle with accepting this purpose, consider that your judgments and unloving thoughts about others and yourself will delay your happiness. If you still cannot let the judgments go, ask for Divine help to learn the value of this worthy goal.

The time spent preparing for an external change in this way will ensure that the change is in your best interest. If you discover after preparing in this way that you no longer have a strong urge to change, you have found the answer to your question. If the desire to move on remains, you have found the answer to your question.

"What would you share to help us when we are experiencing deep despair or extreme fear?"

I am momentarily concerned that these questions are my attempt to control the outcome. I then realize that the questions are part of the channeled message. It occurs to me that they appear as MY questions to encourage my cooperation in receiving the next teaching.

These experiences of utter darkness can be the catalyst to discovering joy and peace, depending on how you respond to these experiences. Your willingness to explore all levels of consciousness is a great strength you possess. However, remaining in these experiences of darkness for any length of time can weaken your awareness of your inherent strength. You might begin to believe that the experience is more powerful than you are. Yet, it is your strength that has led you to these experiences; therefore, it is your strength that leads you out.

When you acknowledge the strength you possess to experience all aspects of yourself, you naturally feel more empowered, less afraid, and lighter.

The beauty of your will and the strength to explore all levels of consciousness are aspects to be admired. When you judge your experience, you deny yourself the love you deserve. If you lose perspective of your strength and love for yourself, ask for Divine help to remember the truth about yourself. You are never without the help you need to learn who you are. Your desire to know the truth of your loving nature aligns you with the help you are receiving and lets you recognize it is an answer you want and need. Using this practice, all experiences, including ones of deep despair and extreme fear, can lead you to great joy.

"Thank you."

February 26

"Good morning. I am ready, open, and willing. What would you share with us now?"

I see the word "love." Receiving this word at the beginning of every message relaxes me and helps me remain open to the message for the day.

I always show you the word "love" to remind you of how important it is to remember your purpose before engaging in any spiritual practice. If you are motivated by something other than love, it is easy to lose your way.

There seem to be other important reasons for engaging in spiritual activities and studies. For instance, you might feel tired, weary, and alone in your quest to escape problems. You might finally realize that your way does not work to solve your problems for good. You might seek freedom from the limitations the world imposes on you. You might want to find a way to experience what you believe will make you happy in this world. You might want peace after experiencing constant stress. You might want a gentle way after straining to get your way. All of these reasons can motivate you to learn something new. What a wonderful moment when you decide to make a discovery! These reasons can be helpful to get you started, yet they will not lead you where you want to go.

I speak to you of love to remind you of the most important reason to learn something new. When learning expands your awareness of pure love, you have made an important discovery. You will know you have discovered pure love when you see, feel, and sense it everywhere, regardless of who or what is there. When you remember that your desire to experience this all-encompassing love is why you explore unconscious beliefs, practice forgiveness, study spiritual texts, and are honest with yourself about what disturbs your peace, you remain highly motivated to reach your goal.

Today's topic will cover some questions that might arise when you practice these teachings to reach your goal. During times of distress, you might notice a tendency to get caught up in the content of the present moment and forget the goal of your practice. That is why I am reminding you of WHY you practice these teachings. When you remember what you are searching for in every moment, you align your practice with the goal.

When you are afraid and want to apply these teachings AND remember that what you seek is the experience of pure love—all that you do to free yourself from fear aligns with your goal. You are less inclined to run or make demands for the world to change and more willing to go within to seek a better understanding of what you fear. You feel empowered to move away from your fearful ideas and toward the love experience you seek.

When you are embarrassed or feel guilty and remember that you want to experience pure love, you instantly realize the judgments you have made upon yourself are moving you away from what you want. You honor instead of judge yourself by asking Divine wisdom to help you see yourself from a loving point of view.

When you are upset because of what someone said or did and remember that you want to experience pure love, you recognize and accept only thoughts and solutions that allow you to see them and yourself lovingly.

It is tempting to forget that love is the experience you seek in these moments. There might be a strong desire to hold on to upset, anger, guilt, or fear, believing this experience is what you want. If you find yourself tempted to think there is a benefit to holding on to the opposite of love, do not fight against this temptation. Allow yourself to fully experience what you believe will offer you safety, love, and freedom. After a while, it will become obvious that this experience is not what you want. What a wonderful discovery!

Be aware of another temptation that can occur. You might be tempted to believe that only others or the world can give you the experience of love. If this occurs, you forget that you are a light being free to experience all levels of consciousness within this present moment, including pure love. Do not reprimand yourself because you have forgotten this fact. Simply see your external seeking as a problem in forgetfulness. What a wonderful thing to remember!

You might then notice a tendency to believe it is impossible to experience pure love in your current circumstance. A little faith at this juncture will serve you well. Faith is believing before you see it or feel it. Amid your current experience remember what it is that you want to experience and have faith! In this way, you honor all experiences without judgment and remain ready, open, and willing to experience something new. When you do, you will discover something amazing!

"Thank you."

∽

PRESENT MOMENT MANTRA
The purpose of this moment is to experience pure love.

MORNING AND BEDTIME MANTRA
I honor all of my experiences as part of my journey.
I am never without Divine help and strength to carry me
through every moment until I discover ever-present love.

February 27

"These teachings can be difficult to practice when we are convinced our unhappiness is due to challenging circumstances, events, or people. Solutions that do not involve changing people or circumstances seem to take us away from happiness, not toward it. Can you address this issue so we do not misunderstand the teachings and delay our happiness?"

This question is important to answer so that you can be clear when you are sabotaging your happiness. Of course, you don't believe you are making yourself unhappy. You think you are doing what needs to be done to ensure your happiness. I will answer this question so that you can be sure your choices lead you to freedom and joy.

Please remember that taking action is neither "good" nor "bad." Also, remember that actions do not necessarily solve the problem of your unhappiness. When you allow a change of mind and heart before taking action, you maximize the potential for the action to be truly helpful and bless everyone involved. If you take action only to serve your interests without consideration for others' happiness and peace, the action will distress you. At first, it might appear that you have gained the upper hand, but you have only managed to prevent yourself from experiencing love and joy.

You can only truly be happy when you experience unity, connection, and love with all creation. If you can change your mind about what you want to gain and include harmony, connection, and love, your actions can help get you what you want. The key to remember is this: What you truly want is an internal experience that can be gained regardless of others' behaviors or agendas.

You can interact within one level of consciousness while being aware of other levels, including the level where unity, love, and connection are obvious. When you maintain this expanded awareness while interacting with life's events and circumstances, all actions become a living, breathing expression of this unity, connection, and love. It will also be the energy of your words, feelings, suggestions, and behaviors.

"Can you give us a practical application of this teaching?"

When you are uncomfortable, upset, angry, or dissatisfied with the current circumstance, remember two things:

1. You want the result to be a blessing for all involved and to honor everyone's right to experience joy and freedom while living in this world.

2. Your happiness and peace result from YOUR experience of unity, connection, and love.

Now that the tone has been set before taking action, you might wonder what to do with your feelings and judgments. I've shared these instructions with you in a previous message. Simply acknowledge your thoughts and emotions and be willing to feel and think differently. You do not have to conjure up a change of heart and mind. It is enough that you recognize your desire for change. Let the actual shift occur through Divine intervention. Your task is to notice the difference and be grateful that it has occurred through your desire to be happy and free.

You have heard it said, "Love your neighbor as yourself." I have given you a way to do this in times of struggle and discord. If you want everyone to benefit from your actions, if you want everyone to know their own worth, and if you want everyone to experience love, then your actions will be a way to love everyone AS you love yourself.

"Thank you."

March 4

I took time off to care for a family member. While tending to their physical and emotional needs, I applied these teachings and experienced some peaceful present moments. As I settle in this morning to resume my routine of receiving messages, my eyes well up with tears.

"Is there more to gain from an experience even though the moment has passed? I am eager to hear today's message."

Life's experiences are meant to be explored to their fullest potential to teach you life's most valuable lessons. Even when fully present in the experience, these lessons might occur to you over time. To be present in the moment requires you to turn off your analytical mind, which enables you to experience everything the moment offers you. When you have time to reflect on the moment, you might become aware of many things you hadn't noticed before. It is like rewinding a movie so you can experience it frame by frame. As you pause to review a scene from your past, you can now take in the whole experience.

I see an image of the cover page of Highlights for Children Magazine. Then, I see the hidden picture page where symbols are concealed within the drawing. I am instructed to look for a banana in the jungle scene. At first, I don't see it. Suddenly, I spot the banana nestled in the tree trunk.

The lesson is that you don't spot the symbol until you know what you are looking for. As you review the experience, look for the love that was in the picture all along. You might have had a sense of love while experiencing the moment, yet now you can focus on and fully appreciate everything about it. You will know you are focusing on love when you feel gratitude and appreciation for the love that is deep within you. If you find yourself anxious or upset when reviewing the experience, allow the feelings to flow while desiring to become aware of the inner love that was present yet remained hidden at the time. Let your mind wander naturally to discover what you might have missed because of the shadow of pain.

If you cannot notice anything but pain in the experience, that is okay. Loving yourself in moments of pain IS discovering the love. If that is all you can do while reviewing this life experience, know it is enough.

This practice enables you to let overwhelming life experiences become moments that, over time, can teach you who you really are.

"Thank you."

March 5

Living in this world requires you to be attentive to your surroundings. This attentiveness is essential because it allows you to be an agent of change within a world that could use a breath of fresh air. The world has lost sight of its purpose: to teach you that YOU are its hope for renewal and rebirth. When you forget your relationship with the world and that you are an agent of change, you experience hopelessness and fatigue. When you remember your purpose in the world, you bring a spark of energy to your life. Life is meant to be enjoyed, yet this cannot be accomplished without you exercising your power as an agent of change.

You have the ability to experience all levels of consciousness. What teaches you the most about who you are is the experience of your power to change the world. Your hesitancy in exploring your inherent power is due to your fear of change. You WILL accept change if it appears to occur due to an external force. Accepting change that occurs due to your internal power seems scary to you.

What would it be like if you decided you no longer wanted to experience a certain feeling, and suddenly, your feeling changed? If it is clear that the change occurred, not as a result of a change in your circumstance, but as a result of your decision, would you rejoice? Or would you deny this natural occurrence, explain it away, or make it seem inconsequential? You see, accepting the truth of who you are is not so easy. That is why I am giving you a gentle approach to self-discovery.

Today's message points to the one who chooses rather than exploring what you choose. We have discussed the many experiences available to you within all levels of consciousness. Learning how to allow your awareness to expand to include all experiences available to you IS an essential part of what I am teaching you. These experiences might seem like they flow in and out of your awareness by some unseen force. Now, it is important to let go of the idea that an external force is determining your internal experience, even if it is associated with a spiritual energy. YOU are this spiritual energy that determines what level of consciousness you will experience at any moment.

Remember what I taught in a previous message about what makes up an experience. The ability to love, feel, and perceive creates the experience. I am reminding you of this teaching because the tendency is to judge the form. This judgment is not helpful to you, nor is it loving to yourself. Let us focus on love, feeling, and perception when I speak to you about you as the decider of your experience.

When you are ready, here is an exercise that will help you know this aspect of yourself:

1. Throughout the day, notice what you perceive and feel in any moment. If you are drawn to focus on the external world, simply turn your attention inward and reflect on your internal experience. Permit yourself to become fully aware of what you perceive and feel without judgment.

2. Call to mind a memory that conjures up feelings of joy and love—a memory when you perceived yourself, others, and the world favorably. Savor the feelings and then ask yourself if you want the same experience now.

3. When you authentically know your answer is yes, decide to have the same experience in your current circumstance. Disregard the mind's chatter about how this change is impossible or cannot occur unless the world, others, or circumstances change by simply returning to the memory that easily brings what you want to your awareness.

There is nothing more you need to do except become conscious of the change occurring as a natural result of your decision. This exercise is a simple, gentle way to begin to accept yourself as an agent of change.

"Thank you."

March 6

Today's message is a continuation of yesterday's teaching.

You might believe you are sacrificing happiness when practicing yesterday's exercise. You might fear you will lose what you want to gain. When you realize there is no gain in making demands on the world to change for you to be happy, you will see that I am leading you toward happiness.

"Why would we want the world to have all the power to determine whether we feel happy?"

Logically, this does not make sense. To believe that others have the power to determine your state of mind and heart renders you powerless. Why would you want to be at the mercy of the world's whims? You don't really want this, but you convince yourself you do because the alternative is unfavorable to you.

The alternative is that you can change your intention and focus in any present moment. This idea frightens you because it ignites unconscious guilt. This fear convinces you to give your power away to an external force. You then add another layer of belief on top of the belief that you are powerless. You believe that to release others and the world of the responsibility to make you happy will result in sacrificing what you want. This double layer of defense hides the truth of your power from your awareness.

Change is the nature of experiences in this world. Desire is the mechanism of change. A change in experience does not change who you are. You are a pure being of light. Regardless of what you perceive and feel, you do not have the power to change who you are. This fundamental confusion about what you can

80

change is the reason for your guilt. To experience love when you once felt fear does not alter the truth. It merely points to an aspect of the truth, which is your ability to experience all levels of consciousness in one present moment.

As you peel back the layers of beliefs, you discover you had the power all along. You might feel uncomfortable, unsettled, resistant, and fearful until you make this discovery. If you have this experience while practicing yesterday's exercise, lovingly remind yourself it is because you are facing the layers of defense put in place to protect your awareness from your power. Remind yourself that you are free and safe to become aware and to feel all aspects of self-discovery. This reminder will help minimize the effects of the beliefs as you look at them and decide not to rebelieve them.

It's best not to fight against the experience of these beliefs or pretend that you do not believe them. Feeling uncomfortable, unsettled, resistant, or fearful indicates that the beliefs are there. What a wonderful moment of self-discovery because you acknowledge what blocks the awareness of who you are. Spend a moment feeling amazed at what your readiness, openness, and willingness have uncovered.

I recall a time when I uncovered a deeply rooted, painful belief. Instead of chastising myself, I chuckled and exclaimed, "I didn't know THAT belief was there!"

A little humor goes a long way in learning how to be free.

By now, you might have noticed that the message I give today is also an exercise in knowing yourself as an agent of change. You are changing your beliefs, feelings, and perceptions through your direction and willingness. Yesterday's exercise might feel more gentle, while today's exercise might feel a bit more uncomfortable. It doesn't matter which feeling you experience. It all leads to the same discovery: You, as a spiritual being, are a powerful agent of change. When you accept this aspect of yourself, you will naturally wonder how you can be truly helpful to the world. The world will be grateful to you because it needs your light and love.

"Thank you."

℀

Present Moment Mantra
I am free and safe to become aware of every aspect of myself,
including my power to choose.

Morning and Bedtime Mantra
As a spiritual being and powerful agent of change,
I am ready, open, and willing to discover how
I can be truly helpful to the world.

March 7

"Is there anything we need to explore further to help us use our life experiences to become a wise, peaceful, loving presence in the world?"

What you hope to gain from any life experience must be decided initially. Notice that within your question is your purpose. You want to know how to use life experiences to gain wisdom and become a peaceful, loving presence in the world. In your previous life experiences, what were you hoping to gain? Pause to review a few of your past life experiences and notice the results you were hoping for.

I pause and review a few experiences from my past. I examine each one and contemplate what I had hoped to gain from the experience.

Becoming wise means seeking a new understanding or an expanded view that is different from what you know now. This requires you to be open to learning something new. When you review your past life experiences, are you open, or do you think you know exactly what is going on, what will solve the problem, what you need, what others need, and what are considered acceptable answers?

To become a peaceful presence in the world means you are willing to let go of anger, hate, judgment, and fear. When you review your past life experiences, is this the case? Or are you seeking peace by demanding the world change, believing that the world is disturbing your peace?

Becoming a loving presence in the world requires you to love yourself first and second, not to exclude anyone from your love. You see everyone, including yourself, as spiritual beings who deserve love and are love itself. When you review your past life experiences, are you chastising yourself? Are you critical of your decisions and actions? Are you willing to look past others' mistakes and acknowledge that their true essence is love?

Now, let us return to the present and the question of how to use your life experiences to become a wise, peaceful, and loving presence in the world. This question indicates a willingness to move forward in your life differently. You have gained awareness of the value of this state-of-being and what a gift it is to yourself and the world.

You have also recognized the value of reviewing past experiences to discover the stumbling blocks that can occur when applying these teachings to all your present moments. Now, if they creep into your present-moment practice, you will notice that an opposing desire has challenged the purpose. This recognition will allow you to stay firm with your purpose and not take the bait. In this way, even past life experiences can become present teachable moments. It enables you to break the patterns of the past in the present in a kind and gentle way.

Love is always trying to find a way into your experience. Even if a door is closed, the light will shine through any crack or opening. Love always finds a way for you to know that it is there. Remember this when you practice these teachings. You don't have to practice perfectly. You merely need to provide some opening for love to shine through. Love was there in the past. Love is here in the present. And love will continue to exist in the future. You practice to expand your awareness of what exists always. You know you have practiced well when you sense even just a sliver of pure love.

"Thank you."

March 8

Love is the reason why you listen and share. We began these teachings with this statement to remind you that love is all that matters in any circumstance, situation, or event. You need constant reminders of what is valuable to you in this world.

This world provides many experiences that are available for your enjoyment. In the game of life, you move ahead on the squares, exploring all that life has to offer. Yet, the experience that offers the most enjoyment and is the most valuable is the awareness of Divine love.

In this world, it is challenging to remember how enjoyable and exciting it is to experience Divine love. You seek out other experiences for the thrill of the ride. The twists and turns and the ups and downs of the ride seem exhilarating and enjoyable, even though you feel a twinge of fear or a sudden loss of stability. You believe these experiences are valuable and that the experience of Divine love is boring. Through mental and emotional conditioning, you have forgotten that you truly value the constancy of love and unwavering peace. That is why you need reminders of why you experience life at all.

You experience life to express the energy of love as thoughts, feelings, sensations, and physical forms. When you experience what is invisible and eternal as a mental, emotional, or physical expression, you catch a glimpse of who you are. These expressions are a way for you to know your Self. When you think, see, or feel this love, you can step back, observe, and declare, "Hey, that's me!"

By now, you might have realized that my teachings use all life experiences to aid you in self-discovery. You might not believe that you want to discover who you are in this life. Regardless of whether you are aware of this desire, it is your life's purpose. Most, if not all, would at least acknowledge that they are pursuing happiness, love, safety, comfort, fulfillment, freedom from worry, acceptance, and belonging. These qualities are the essence of who you are. When you experience any one of these qualities, you are discovering an aspect of yourself.

What you want to experience in this life must be honored and acknowledged as valuable to you. The reason why it is valuable might elude you temporarily, yet eventually, you see the correlation between these experiences and a spiritual journey of self-discovery. Nurture the desire to have your life become a living, breathing expression of these beautiful qualities of your spiritual nature. Beware of the temptation to diminish the importance of these qualities, believe you are undeserving, or that it is selfish to want to experience life in this way. If you give in to this temptation, you deny yourself the joy of self-discovery, and you teach others that life is not meant to be joyful.

In life, you are either experiencing these qualities or experiencing the opposite of these qualities. When experiencing these beautiful aspects of who you are, respond with gratitude and appreciation for what life is teaching you. When experiencing the opposite of these qualities, respond with gratitude and appreciation for the opportunity to know yourself better.

Honor your desire to experience the qualities of your spiritual nature by choosing to let life teach you who you really are. The changes you experience due to this choice can occur quickly or over time, depending on how much resistance there is to change.

I see an image of a large ship about fifty miles from shore. The captain turns the wheel to the left. The ship turns slowly due to its vast size and the resistance created by the water. Only the slight changes in the landscape indicate that the ship is turning.

With every slight change you notice, give gratitude to yourself for your willingness to play the game of life and honor all experiences along the way.

"Thank you."

PART II

Dissolving Difficulties

Difficulties are opportunities to change your experience
from a limited view of the shadow of pain
to an expanded awareness of Divine love.

NESHEA

March 9

Part II of my teachings will focus on your devotion to your purpose and the difficulties that can arise when you implement these teachings as part of your devotion. Once you become 100% devoted, the difficulties in using life experiences as a vehicle to experience your true nature melt away. Highlighting the difficulties and learning how to meet them with gentleness and love will complete your devotion to your purpose. To think that you will not have any difficulties in applying these teachings to your life experiences is not in your best interest. It would be better for you to approach your practice with humbleness and complete honesty.

You fear that when you experience difficulties, you are a failure. You believe that any resistance you experience on your spiritual journey means you are not worthy of help and support. That is why you pretend to be a devoted student and ignore or deny that you have trouble with your devotion. You believe that any wavering in your practice makes you less than worthy in the eyes of your Creator. You fear you will be judged rather than supported in this moment of difficulty. As a result, you try to overcome difficulties through perseverance and hard work, which makes the journey arduous and lengthy.

I want to teach you how to embrace the difficulties and make them part of the plan to receive all the gifts that are inherently yours. Therefore, we will embark on a journey of deep exploration into the difficulties you encounter on your spiritual path. When you learn to transform difficulties into joy, you will be 100% devoted to your life's purpose.

I speak to you of devotion because, as a spiritual being, anything that you truly want without reservation or hesitation, you will allow yourself to have. This means you are willing to receive all the gifts being offered to you in every present moment. You are much more willing to explore the joys of a spiritual path than you are willing to explore the difficulties you encounter along the way. If you trust me, I will lead you gently toward the difficulties and through them. I have your best interest at heart and know what you need to enjoy every moment life offers you.

Difficulties are opportunities to change your experience from a limited view of the shadow of pain to an expanded awareness of Divine love. When you learn that every moment can be miraculous, you will not have difficulty remaining devoted to your purpose.

"Thank you."

March 10

In Part I, we discussed many of the challenges you face when exploring the present moment and how to accept each challenge and overcome them through grace. The difficulties we will address now are similar in nature, but they also contain elements of resistance that, when they go unnoticed, can create chaos in your life.

Difficulties are not necessarily the same as challenges. Challenges occur when you are committed to the goal and the means, yet you find that specific points require more tenacity and willingness to keep going. Difficulties occur when you question if the goal is worthy of your time and attention and believe the means are taking you away from what you desire. Difficulties, therefore, need to be handled quite differently from how you meet challenges because the essence of the practice is believed NOT to be what you want.

The essence is, of course, the discovery of your true nature. This discovery entails all aspects of who you are, including but not limited to your ability to love, feel, perceive, and experience all creation as it is in truth. This goal threatens your current self-concept. If you believe that letting go of who you think you are is a loss of self, you will waiver on practicing the means to achieve the ultimate goal of your life. That is why difficulties, when encountered, can turn you in the opposite direction, while challenges merely delay your progress.

I am here to help you remain devoted to your path by addressing these difficulties with clarity, precision, and fortitude. It is essential that you approach this exploration with curiosity and gratitude. When you judge your fears and beliefs that tempt you to retreat and go back to old ways, you are most unloving to yourself. If you let me point out the difficulties, I will do so lovingly and respectfully because you deserve the utmost love, honor, and respect.

Any spiritual practice that involves judgment will merely set you back and delay your experience of joy and love. Do not convince yourself that judgment is necessary to achieve results. A simple way to overcome the temptation to use judgment as a means to progress is to replace a "judgment" with a "thank you." For instance, when you say to yourself, "I should have known better. Why can't I make a better choice?" Replace this judgment with, "I am grateful for my willingness to notice what I am choosing and to learn what choice will bring me joy."

There is always something to be grateful to yourself for in your life experiences. Notice that I did not say to be grateful FOR the external circumstance, event, or situation. The external can be noticed and appreciated because it offers you an opportunity to experience your true nature. However, when you can love yourself even in a difficult situation, you are ALREADY experiencing your true nature.

This simple practice of replacing a judgmental thought with a thought of gratitude to yourself will help you through all difficulties. Therefore, I ask you to engage in this practice for at least one day to experience the benefits before moving on to the following message.

March 11

Devotion to your purpose and the means to fulfill your purpose are the essential ingredients needed to become aware of all that exists in the present moment. If either is threatened by a misunderstanding that love and unity are not what you want, your devotion and practice will not yield results. In contrast, if you know that what you gain through devotion and practice is all you could ever want and need, you will have instant success.

What you don't want to realize is how easy it is to gain all you want in the moment you are in. You insist it is difficult to feel and perceive anything different than what you are experiencing at that moment. You maintain this belief to safeguard your perceived reality, believing that it can still provide you some relief. Yet, deep down, you know how easy it is to open your eyes and see everything. Let's take a moment and see if this is true.

Close your eyes. Notice how limited your view of the world is with your eyes closed. Now, open your eyes. Look at all that you missed because your eyes were closed! How difficult was it to open your eyes? This is how easy it is to expand your awareness to encompass all levels of consciousness—including the awareness of who you really are. That is not to say you do not experience difficulties practicing these teachings. However, we must be clear about WHAT is difficult if we are to make it easier for you to practice.

To acknowledge that it is not difficult to experience expanded awareness and become universally conscious is very helpful to you. Can you do so now with sincerity? Pause and reflect on this truth: It is easy to perceive all levels of consciousness and to experience my true nature. Do you accept this statement as the truth, even if you are still unsure how it is accomplished? If the answer is "no," express gratitude to yourself for your honesty. Then ask yourself, "Why do I want it to be difficult to experience my true nature?" When you ask this question with sincerity, you realize that you DO want it to be easy, even if your experience so far has been challenging.

Your heart's desire is stronger than your current beliefs and experiences. Therefore, when you are tempted to maintain your version of reality, focus on the fact that you want it to be easy to experience joy, peace, fulfillment, safety, and love. Remember, I am teaching you how to be free and happy while you experience living in this world. This state-of-being expands to influence and help others to be free and happy, too. If you believe that what you devote time and energy to will not lead to freedom and happiness, you will either leave it behind or continue in despair. You choose all your endeavors based on this litmus test.

When you decide that something will result in greater freedom and happiness, you deem it worthy of your time and attention. In addition, you are willing to face and move past challenges and difficulties you encounter along the way. When what you choose does not give you the results you were hoping for, you reevaluate and choose again. Let us use this natural way of decision-making to your benefit.

You might choose a judgment, a hateful thought, or a grievance because you believe it will result in greater freedom and happiness. When you evaluate what you have gained from this choice, you recognize it has failed to give you what you want. Now, it becomes easy to let it go and choose again. Likewise, you might notice that attempts to achieve greater freedom and happiness from people, places, and things result in less than you were hoping for. Realizing that your efforts yield little results, you are willing to try something new.

You have heard it said, "First within, then without," meaning both internal and external combine to complete the experience.

Achieving external results without a congruent internal experience results in complacency. To achieve an internal experience of freedom and happiness without it affecting your perception of the external world is impossible. Any teaching that leads you toward a change of mind and heart is guiding you to greater freedom and happiness. This change can be measured by examining the results of your practice.

Once you accept the possibility that these teachings can result in greater freedom and happiness, you are willing to look closely at the difficulties you might encounter along the way. Spend time throughout the day contemplating the idea that what you are learning can guide you to greater freedom and happiness. Notice if your level of devotion increases. Are you more willing to devote time and energy to your practice? Are you willing to look closely at the difficulties and learn how to overcome them? This contemplation exercise is a beautiful and loving way to give your whole heart and mind to your practice, which, as I said before, are the essential ingredients needed to gain the results you are hoping for.

"Thank you."

March 12

In the message given on March 9th, I made a point to clarify why you deny the difficulties you have when asked to use the present moment for expanded awareness. Denial is a powerful defense that prevents you from experiencing freedom and joy in the present moment. Making yourself aware of what you are denying creates extreme conflict. You push forward, and then you pull back, not sure if you want to know what you are denying. Instead of approaching it this way, I offer a gentler approach to help you be honest with yourself.

I ask you to return to the paragraph explaining what having difficulties means to you. As you read the paragraph, notice what statements ring true for you.

I found and re-read the paragraph referenced in the message from March 9th:

"You fear that when you experience difficulties, you are a failure. You fear that any resistance you experience on your spiritual journey means you are not worthy of help and support. That is why you pretend to be a devoted student and ignore or deny that you have trouble with your devotion. You believe that any wavering in your practice makes you less than worthy in the eyes of your Creator. You fear you will be judged rather than supported in this moment of difficulty. As a result, you try to overcome the difficulties through perseverance and hard work, which makes the journey arduous and lengthy."

Upon reflection, I realize that I have thought these things about myself.

Once you realize that you have these fears and hold these beliefs, you now have an opportunity to accept Divine help. Knowing that you won't be judged, you are ready to acknowledge that you ARE having difficulty practicing these teachings. And, you naturally become curious to learn the reason WHY you are having difficulty.

Ultimately, you are in conflict about what will bring you freedom and happiness in the present moment. This struggle is why you have difficulty giving 100% of your time and attention to expanding your awareness to include the true nature of all creation.

I see an image of a marathon race. I stand at the starting line, hesitant to begin because I'm not sure it is worth the effort to reach the finish line. My coach stands before me, describing the joy I will experience when I reach my goal. He promises that the rewards are well worth the effort.

The coach can make this promise because he has run the race before. He has crossed the finish line and reaped the rewards. He speaks with conviction because he knows what he speaks of is the truth. You, on the other hand, might have run shorter distances and experienced some happiness, but what he speaks of is beyond any experience you have had so far. You wonder if you should just be content with the small rewards. You consider stepping out of the race altogether. Maybe it would be better to return to your old life and ways of solving problems and forget that you ever had a chance to reach such a goal.

There is no right or wrong decision. We discussed this teaching before. You cannot completely deny yourself your heart's desire. Eventually, you will participate in the race and achieve your goal. Yet, at this moment, I ask you to be fully aware of your decision without judgment or condemnation. Review your choices and be honest about your concerns. Then, ask for Divine help in deciding what you are ready for.

Even if you go back to solving problems the old way, you have learned a great deal about yourself. You have expanded your awareness to include other choices you did not see before. You have learned to make decisions without putting yourself down for the decisions you make. You have learned you are not alone and have loving Divine help and guidance to support you without judgment. You might even look upon the world differently, realizing that the world is a wonderful place to learn about yourself.

If you decide to be content with these rewards, you have cause to rejoice. You have learned how to use the present moment to become aware of your feelings and thoughts instead of repressing them. You have learned how to be honest with yourself instead of pretending you are not where you are. This honesty becomes an incredible learning feat when you are honest while continuing to love yourself and appreciate the experience you are having.

You might even have learned how to have compassion for others who are displaying their inner conflict and pain. To soften your heart toward others when they are not expressing their best selves helps release your anger and judgment. This change of heart is a reward in and of itself. You naturally feel better when you feel compassion.

If you are content with what you have learned and decide this change is all you are ready for, then continue to practice this way. Running these small races and reaping the benefits helps you become ready for what comes next. When you decide that you are ready to achieve the ultimate reward of expanded awareness in the present moment, you will have all the help you need to reach your goal.

At the beginning, middle, or end, you might experience difficulties committing to the goal. As your coach, I will address these difficulties and help you through them. If you have come this far, be assured that you ARE ready. I am here with you and will help you achieve your goal.

"Thank you."

March 21

I have highlighted the main difficulty you have in practicing these teachings. Your concern is that what you gain from your practice will not be what you want. Therefore, what you gain is not worth the effort. If not addressed, this concern will result in a lack of readiness to practice these teachings in your present moments. I have asked you to be honest about your concerns. Honesty is the first step in dissolving the difficulty. Now, we will specifically address the belief that YOU know what you want and need to experience freedom and joy.

You ask for specific experiences because you believe they will bring you happiness and make the ride more thrilling. Yet, you often feel afraid, lonely, unfulfilled, and dissatisfied with your experience. You then seek out another experience that you believe will result in greater freedom and happiness. When this experience fails to give you what you want, you try even harder to figure out what you want.

This dissatisfaction with your current experience can increase your willingness to try new things. Many have begun a spiritual journey from this condition of dissatisfaction and willingness. At this juncture, you have clarity about what you desire to experience. You have learned how much you value the experience of profound peace, all-encompassing love, and a deep connection with everyone and everything. Yet, you are confused about WHAT will provide you with this experience. When you have difficulty practicing spiritual teachings, it is not because you are confused about what you want to experience. You are having trouble believing that your spiritual practice will give you the desired experience.

Honesty is crucial here. I ask you to voice your concerns and be specific about what you think will provide you with the desired experience. Some of the ideas might be divinely inspired.

Some ideas might originate from an old way of solving problems. Therefore, I ask you to be specific without judgment but also without righteousness. Remaining flexible and open-minded while remaining firmly committed to the experience you desire will help you dissolve the difficulty you have in being led along the way. When your spiritual practice manifests the desired experience, and you witness its expression in the world, any difficulty you have at the starting line will dissolve completely.

In conclusion, everyone's path must be honored as a living expression of their Divine creative nature. This acceptance can be difficult when you are unaware of all levels of consciousness, including the ultimate realization of who you are. Yet, if you resist or deny any expression of your divinity, you limit your understanding and view of the whole.

A simple way to dissolve this difficulty is to allow all experiences into your awareness without judgment.

1. Feel and perceive all you can in the present moment, regardless if it is "good" or "bad." At the same time, acknowledge that what you feel and perceive are only aspects of the whole. This recognition will help you stay present without limiting yourself to your current experience.

   + If the experience is unpleasant or uncomfortable, be aware of the tendency to accept what you currently feel and see as the ONLY option available. To help you overcome this limitation, remember everyone's right, including your own, to experience expansive love, peace, and joy.

2. Acknowledge that you do not know what will bring you and others the experience everyone deserves. Remain open to Divine intervention.

   + If any concerns arise about what you will gain or lose, be honest about your concerns and ask for Divine help.

This practice is how you dissolve all difficulties gently and lovingly.

"Thank you."

March 22

When you hear me speak of a way to freedom and joy, you listen with great interest and care on behalf of yourself and others. You begin to wonder what your present experience would be like if you were to practice these teachings. You look ahead and try to predict your future life experiences if you expand your awareness in the present moment. You try to envision the future because it is difficult to surrender to something unfamiliar. The trouble is that you have no frame of reference to perceive what lies ahead. This lack of context produces an uneasy feeling because you are unsure if the results of your practice will be beneficial.

Take a moment and see if you can imagine what comes next after an experience of expanded awareness.

I pause and look ahead. I cannot visualize or conjure what a future moment would be like if I were to experience expanded awareness in the present moment. I feel unsettled and nervous.

You might waver in your determination and focus when you cannot see the results. You might slip into old ways of responding to the present moment because you find comfort in the familiar. Try to remember that all future moments result from decisions made in the present. When you stay focused and determined to apply these teachings to your current life experience, you can experience a future that is better than the past.

Remember, you cannot properly evaluate your choices until you see their results. You, first, must make the choice and then evaluate the choice based on the outcome. The outcome is unknown to you in the present moment. Yet, you are still asked to choose even if you cannot see the results. Be focused and determined to make a choice. Then use the results to learn whether you want to continue to make the same choice in the next present moment. This experiential way of learning allows you to make choices with greater freedom and less judgment. Your choices and their results become a way for you to choose what you want to experience wisely.

For example, let us say that you are in a present moment that you find distasteful. The world is not giving you what it is you want to feel safe and happy. You think you know what is best for you in the present moment and the future. When you are not getting what you want, you have a choice. How will you respond? Will you apply what I have been teaching you or return to old ways of responding?

As you pause to make this choice, you naturally look ahead to see the results of each choice before you decide. The choice to respond in the old way leads to a result that you can see clearly, if you are willing to be honest about the past. In other words, a fantasy of what you hoped would have happened due to your choice is not helpful. Look to the past and see what resulted from your choice. Did you experience pure love, connection, and joy? Did you experience a friendlier world, a helpful world, a world that loves and cares for you?

Now, let us return to your second choice, which is to apply the teachings I shared with you. When you look ahead at the results, you cannot imagine what they would be. Unless, of course, in the past, you chose to apply these teachings to your life experience. If you did so in the past, I guarantee it was a beneficial outcome. If this is the case, it is easy to make the same choice in your present circumstance. If you did not make this choice in the past, then make the choice now with determination and focus. If you feel resistance, go ahead and do what you must do. There is no judgment, only learning. You can learn from any choice you make.

No matter what you choose, you can learn by its results, which is how you gently lead yourself to the experience you want to have. The world is here for you to learn just that.

"Thank you."

March 23

Old ways are hard to break. Yet, leaving the old for something new is the essence of expanded awareness.

I see an image of circles within circles within circles. In between each circle is a line. The lines connect one circle to another circle.

You are given a bridge to move from one level of consciousness to another. This bridge helps you leave one level of awareness to embrace a more expanded view of the present moment. Each change in awareness involves a change in feelings, perceptions, and understanding of love. If you are unwilling to leave past feelings, perceptions, and beliefs behind, nothing new can be experienced. We addressed the importance of letting go in Part I. Now, we will look closely at your difficulty in letting go of the past.

Each experience of feelings, perceptions, and understanding of love solidifies into a self-concept. You embrace each experience and then use it to develop a more comprehensive present view of who you are.

"Can you give us an example, please?"

For instance, let us say that in the past, you experienced betrayal. You perceived the other as separate from you and purposely doing harm to you by acting selfishly. You felt alone, rejected, and abandoned. The love that you felt for this person has turned to hate. If it was your first experience of betrayal, you include all that you felt, perceived, and understood about love into your self-concept. Your understanding of who you are now encompasses the idea that you can be harmed, rejected, and abandoned. Your understanding of love has become one that involves pain. You now perceive others as separate from you and believe their behavior is something you can judge without judging yourself.

Let us say that you grow weary and tired of the experience of betrayal. You decide you want to feel and perceive differently. You decide that your understanding of love needs to change if you want to experience pure love. You want to walk across the bridge to experience something new. There are a few things you must do to cross the bridge. You must let go of who you thought yourself and others to be. You must release the idea that you can be betrayed or harmed, that others are separate from you, and that love involves pain. Would you find this letting go difficult? You might find it difficult because the experience of betrayal has now become a part of who you think you are. Therefore, walking across the bridge can feel like leaving a part of yourself behind.

Let us say that the experience in the past was not negative but positive. For instance, in the past, you stretched yourself to explore a new way of living. You studied new ideas and learned through life experiences that you are strong, competent, and courageous. Your self-concept grew to encompass feelings of self-love and a perception of you as a worthy individual. Now, you understand love in a new way and feel good about yourself. How difficult is it to leave THIS self-concept behind? Yet, you must to expand your awareness beyond what you currently know about yourself.

"In both examples, I can see how letting go of the past would be difficult. What will help us dissolve this difficulty?"

When you are on the bridge, remember that you are always moving toward something better. The more uncomfortable self-concepts are easier to let go of. If you like your current self-concept, you might want to remain at this level of awareness for a while. You might want to rest at this level for enjoyment or to integrate what you have learned about yourself. You can remain at any level of awareness for as long as you like. YOU decide when you are ready to expand.

Once you decide to expand your awareness of who you are, you might travel back and forth between the old and new feelings, perceptions, and understanding about love. Juggling both can create confusion and friction. In one instance, you might feel, perceive, and act from your old self-concept. In another instance, your feelings and perceptions expand, and you see, feel, and act from this expanded self-concept. Accept this way of experiencing transitions as a normal occurrence.

To ease the transition, try to recognize when you are experiencing an old self-concept (an old way of feeling, perceiving, and loving). Without judgment, honor what the old self-concept has brought to you in the past and then give your consent to experience new feelings, perceptions, and understanding about love. Remember, when you expand your awareness, you always move toward something better. This practice can help dissolve the difficulty in letting go of old ways of being and cross the bridge to experience something new.

"Thank you."

March 24

Are you willing to be surprised? Life is not meant to be predictable. Each new moment is unknown until you experience it. It is only after the moment has passed that you can then speak about what it is like. You describe your experiences through emotions, perceptions, and interpretations of what has occurred. How can you describe these things BEFORE you have the experience?

The desire to know what the next moment will be like is an obstacle in receiving the most expanded present-moment experience you are ready for. That is because to predetermine a future experience, you have only past experiences to draw from. Therefore, when you try to predict a future moment, you are actually remembering the past instead of expanding into something new. Let us find a way to step around this obstacle.

In a previous message, I emphasized the problem that you think you know something of importance. Now, we will address your NEED to know. Your need to know comes from a lack of trust and the belief that you will not have what you need if the future moment is a surprise. There is a simple way to gain trust and to learn that you will always have what you need when you arrive at the next present moment.

Recall a moment in your life when you were surprised by the experience you were having. Choose a memory of when you experienced joy with the surprise.

I recall a memory of when I studied abroad. Without any previous experiences of being in a foreign country, every day held multiple wonderful surprises.

A surprise is when you cannot possibly predict what will happen next. And when it does happen, you are amazed. Before you embark on a new adventure which is the next present moment, you might feel nervous not knowing what comes next. This nervousness can be exciting if you allow the possibility that a new present moment can hold many wonderful surprises for you. To ease your fear that you will not have the resources to feel secure, happy, and fulfilled in a new present moment, remind yourself that you can never be alone in any moment you are in. Your inner strength and wisdom are with you in every moment.

To be surprised does not mean you will not have what you need. It means you cannot possibly know what you need UNTIL you are in the present moment. When you recall a memory of when you were pleasantly surprised, did you have all that you needed? Were you given things that you did not even know you needed? Were the emotions beyond what you could have predicted?

When you walk through life wanting to be surprised, you easily move around the obstacle and learn to cross the bridge to expanded levels of consciousness without fear.

"I have experienced unpleasant surprises, such as the unexpected death of my baby daughter. These painful surprises in my life seem to override the pleasant surprises. How can we enter a new present moment with open arms when some of our surprises have been painful?"

Again, I say to you that your inner strength and wisdom are with you every moment. When you experience a painful surprise and then lose the awareness of your strength and wisdom, it is due to a lack of practice in responding to unpredictable events. If you have over-practiced controlling and predicting every future moment and suddenly something occurs that you couldn't foresee, you might feel unsteady and unsure. This reaction merely means you need to practice being fully present in any moment you are in without it uprooting you.

I see an image of a blade of grass moving gently with the wind while remaining firmly rooted in the ground.

Reviewing past painful surprises from this perspective will help you be more determined to practice these teachings.

These teachings give you a firm foundation to experience every present moment, regardless of the circumstance, event, or situation. They have the power to transform even painful surprises into joyful moments. However, painful moments require more trust, vigilance, and faith. To gain these, practice is needed.

I ask you for a little extra willingness to look at your past painful surprises from this perspective so that you do not use them to avoid the joyful surprises that await you in your future present moments.

"Thank you."

March 25

"In the past, I have experienced moments of expanded awareness, which led to miraculous results. When we have profound spiritual experiences of expanded awareness, is it helpful to share them with others, or are they meant to remain private? Why do I feel sad when others do not understand or share in the joy I experienced?"

Your questions have brought to light a major difficulty in allowing your awareness to expand beyond the limited world you see—beyond your limited version of yourself. When experiencing pure love, unity, and undeniable innocence and beauty, you feel as if you have arrived home after a long journey. You now know why you are here and what is the most precious gift you could ever receive while living in this world. To leave this state of mind is to return to the mundane task of survival. Yet, you can never again value the "gifts" the world offers in exchange for all your efforts to survive. You now know WHAT is worth your effort. And you want to capture the joy, love, and unity you experienced while in this expanded state of consciousness.

You believe sharing the details with others will unify this world with the world of expanded awareness. When others listen, however, they have no frame of reference to conceptualize the experience that you speak of. Therefore, they receive the information and squeeze it into a paradigm they can understand. Instead of allowing the sharing to stretch their minds to experience something outside of normal perception, they might mold it into an acceptable and less fearful form. I have spoken to you before about the comfort of the familiar.

This understanding does not mean sharing your experiences with others is not helpful. It means that when you share, you must allow others to receive whatever is most helpful to them. If you experience sadness when others do not honor or share your experience in quite the same way, you misunderstand what unifies you with the whole.

Sadness is derived from the perception of loss and separation. You believe a lack of unified understanding and experience separates you from others. The unity you experienced with expanded awareness is now perceived as lost to you. To regain a sense of connection, you do not have to convince others or have others share your experience. Awareness of unity comes from an expanded awareness of all levels of consciousness. This experience is always available to you in every moment, regardless if one agrees with you or understands what is being shared.

Therefore, to relieve you of the deep sadness you are experiencing, you merely need to cross the bridge from your limited perception and allow a more expanded view of the whole. Your feelings of joy and love will return immediately.

THIS is the way you honor everyone's path, including your own. THIS is how you release others from the burden of giving you the desired experience. THIS is the way you experience freedom in a world that wants to maintain its version of reality. THIS is how you maintain a sense of unity even if your experiences are not understandable to others. THIS is how you remain true to yourself while loving others who are on their own path.

"Thank you for helping me."

March 26

"I continue to struggle with feelings of deep sadness. What would you share with me now?"

As you honor the desire to embrace these teachings, an old wound of loss resurfaces. You challenge the status quo when you leave behind previous beliefs and behaviors and embrace new understandings and responses. When you step out of the familiar and acceptable paradigm, you might leave others behind. There might be those who once shared your point of view but now have a different path to follow. If you are to continue to honor your path, it is essential to be at peace with how others respond to your choices.

"The new me is at peace, but the old me was devastated when following my path meant leaving others behind. I sense that somehow these past experiences continue to influence me."

An old memory can delay a new beginning. To avoid delays, ask to understand the old from a new perspective. When you have expanded awareness, the life that you knew before is gone. You relate to people differently, and they see you differently. Some might want to join you in the direction you are headed. Others will travel down a different path that suits them perfectly. Parting ways does not mean separation. The love that binds you together is ever-present. It might appear that you have been rejected, but I assure you, that is never the case. If you react to their response with anything other than love and compassion, YOU need a healing remedy.

Do not diminish yourself in an effort not to feel the old wounds of separation. Ask yourself instead, "How do I want to be in the world now?"

I ask myself this question. I then see an image of me sharing my experiences, untouched by people's reactions, because I sense our connection, see their beauty, and honor their choices.

Truly, I say to you, others' reactions have nothing to do with you. They are responding to their own internal emotions, thoughts, and perceptions. It is most unhelpful to yourself and others if you are confused about their reaction. When you are not experiencing only love, ask yourself, "How do I want to be in the world now?" If you do not have the experience you want, ask for Divine help, which will be given immediately.

Remember, the way you can be truly helpful in all circumstances and every situation is to acknowledge your internal world and ask for the awareness that sets EVERYONE free.

"Thank you."

PART III

Relationships

*Your relationships are the training ground to
reach amazing heights of awareness.*

NESHEA

March 27

Any teaching that uses the world as a means to realize Divine truth must address the topic of relationships because relationships are the majority of your life experiences. Consider the fundamental definition of a relationship and you will see that your whole life consists of nothing but this type of interaction with the world.

A relationship involves two parts interacting with one another. When two parts make contact, a relationship begins. These relationship experiences range from a subatomic level unseen by the naked eye to the energetic vibration of the Divine Creator interacting with Its creations. What is in between these invisible relationships is what you experience as relationships in your world.

You believe you are in a relationship when interacting with a physical form, whether it be a person, place, or thing. That is because you believe you are a physical being. Relationships have nothing to do with the physical form. They are comprised of the interaction between emotions, thoughts, and perceptions. Because these three intangible elements are present in every moment, you can say you are in a relationship in every moment. Consider how you go about your day, and you will see that this is so.

I recall holding my first cup of coffee in the morning, getting into my car, looking at the scenery as I drive down the road, paying bills, reading Facebook posts, meditating, and receiving these messages.

As you review these moments, notice that emotions, thoughts, and perceptions are present in each one.

I consider each of these moments and notice that feelings, thoughts, and perceptions ARE present.

Now consider the people you meet each day. Pause to become aware of your emotions, thoughts, and perceptions while interacting with the people in your life. It does not matter if they are an acquaintance or a life-long partner. The longevity or importance of the relationship does not determine whether these three elements are present in your experience. It does, however, determine the variations of feelings, thoughts, and perceptions you do have. Regardless, the fact remains that emotions, thoughts, and perceptions are present in every interaction.

When you encounter another part of the whole, your relationship experience is determined by your emotions, thoughts, and perceptions during the interaction. These three things are changeable. And that is why you experience different kinds of relationships in your life. When your awareness expands to include the highest level of consciousness, the emotion is pure love, the thought is Divine truth, and the perception is oneness. When you greet every present moment interaction with this awareness, you will find you have the same relationship with every part of the world. Until then, your relationship experiences will vary. Until then, every relationship can become a means to gain what you want to experience in every present moment.

You believe your relationships trap you in a certain emotion, thought, and perception because the other part of the relationship is not cooperating to give you what you want. When your coffee is cold, your car breaks down; people cut in front of you in line, your computer crashes, your colleague makes a mistake, your friend doesn't return your phone call, or your partner does not listen, you believe the reason why the present moment is unfavorable is that the other part of the relationship is uncooperative. But, when you look closely at the present moment and notice your emotions, thoughts, and perceptions, you can see that these elements are the major contributors to your experience of the relationship in the present moment. This awareness alone can begin to solve many of your relationship issues.

It is tempting to believe that you are powerless to change your experience when interacting with the world. That is why it is helpful to practice this simple awareness exercise during the interaction:

- Notice your emotions, thoughts, and perceptions without judgment.

- Avoid analyzing others' intentions, feelings, and thoughts, which will only delay awareness of your own.

- Be aware of the temptation to believe that what you are interacting with (whether it is a person, place, or thing) must change for your emotions, thoughts, and perceptions to change.

  - You can resist this temptation by returning your awareness to your feelings, thoughts, and perceptions.

- See how long you can maintain this awareness without trying to change anything.

This practice will help you learn to trust your ability to embrace all life experiences without flinching.

You may think staying present during a negative experience will be difficult. Actually, you might find it more difficult to maintain feelings of joy and love. Either way, you are learning that you are not the experience. You are the one who is aware of your experience, and no experience can change who you are.

"Thank you."

March 28

Our true relationship is beyond this world. When you become aware of your true relationship with the universal mind, you have reached a state that you call "heaven." Heaven is the experience of one emotion of pure love, one thought of Divine truth, and one perception of oneness. There is a level of universal consciousness beyond this state. But for our purposes, we will speak of "heaven" as the ultimate level of awareness you can attain while you experience life in this world.

Perceiving oneness seems to be an oxymoron. To perceive, there must be a perceiver and something to be perceived. Oneness indicates a state where there is nothing set apart from itself. When we speak of perception, there are two; when we speak of oneness, there is only one. Therefore, a perception of oneness doesn't make sense. Yet, for our purposes, we will speak of oneness as a state of consciousness where perception is part of the experience. We will do so because the true oneness of creation is a significant leap for those who perceive themselves as a body in this world.

You can take every experience, including one where you perceive yourself walking in this world, as a stepping stone to greater awareness. Once you experience the ultimate level of consciousness, taking the final step to experience true oneness will be effortless. For now, let us be content with what we can achieve in our current condition. The ESSENCE of true oneness can be experienced in this world. The essence of something is not the real thing, yet it can be helpful to lead you to experience what is real and true.

Telepathy, synchronicity, empathy, prophecy, prayer, healing, and channeling are all physical manifestations of the essence of oneness. Tuning into others' thoughts, having prior knowledge of future events, communicating without speaking, being in the right place at the right time, having an awareness of other's emotions, and being a conduit of Divine healing and messages all suggest that what seems like separate parts are actually connected by something invisible. When what you do, think, feel, or say affects a "separate" person, place, or thing, you are learning about your connection to the whole. You are expanding your awareness beyond the physical world to the invisible realm.

These are all wonderful stepping stones that can open your heart and mind to experience a relationship unfamiliar to you. When you are ready to experience this level of connection, regardless of the proximity of the physical form, you are ready to leap toward experiencing your true relationship with the whole. Some pitfalls can be experienced along the way, which we will address. For now, let us honor everything in your life experience that points to your true relationship.

To discover the essence of your true relationship, you must look past the physical form and your present emotions, thoughts, and perceptions. This internal seeing can be done whether the interaction is negative or positive. When interacting with a person, place, or thing, I ask you to notice your emotions, thoughts, and perceptions. Once you have acknowledged them, it is time to see what lies beyond your current experience.

To get a sense of the invisible bond that connects all things, close your eyes and, without striving, see if you can sense this connection. Devoting just a few minutes to experiencing this invisible bond can help you in all your interactions. Any slight sensations of peace, love, and joy are indicators that you are becoming aware. Any physical expressions of this invisible bond can be honored and enjoyed. Experiencing this connection is how your relationships in this world can help you learn the truth of who you are. Practice with joy, even if the interaction is less than joyful. You will soon discover the reason why it is a joyful practice.

In this world, you seem to be connection-deprived. This sense of separation is the cause of much of your sorrow while living in this world. Yet, you can never be disconnected. Some might not like this fact because they do not want to be connected to others' pain and fear. What I am teaching you will bring you only joy because you expand beyond this world to the level of consciousness where all connections are bonds of love. That is why I have asked you to practice the way I have outlined for you. It bypasses the misunderstanding many have that to connect; you must do so with the physical form. That is not to say that experiencing the invisible bond of love will not have a physical expression. Naturally, it does. It is to say that the physical expression will be one of love because that is the essence of the invisible bond.

I ask you to sense this connection first, then open your eyes to the physical world and rejoice at its manifestations. People, places, and things move in and out of your life accordingly, while the bond that connects all things remains intact. This awareness will bring you great joy and peace as you flow through your life experiences.

"Thank you."

March 29

You make many demands on your relationships. You require your relationships to fulfill the needs you believe you have in the present moment. The needs are many, or so you believe. When you perceive that the present moment is empty of connection, love, safety, appreciation, worthiness, honor, gratitude, fulfillment, or a sense of purpose—you interact with a person, place, or thing to get what you need.

Your first reaction to hearing this message might be denial. You maintain that you interact with the world to give and receive love. On a deep level, you know that love is the essence of all living things, and to experience this love is the ultimate reward for all your efforts. I ask you to hold tight to this knowledge and, simultaneously, be honest about how you use relationships to meet your needs. To do so is to return your relationships to their original purpose.

Pause and recall a recent interaction with a person, place, or thing in which you felt something was lacking. Make a note of what you need at that moment. Then, notice what needs you were asking the person, place, or thing to provide for you.

There are only two possible outcomes to your request:

1. You were given everything you needed.

2. The person, place, or thing failed to give you what you needed.

If outcome #1 occurred, you left the moment feeling satisfied and happy. If outcome #2 occurred, you left the moment feeling empty.

You decide whether to keep the person, place, or thing in your life based on the outcome. If it provides what you need, you continue to interact with this aspect of the world. If it fails to provide what you need, you either try again or walk away. When relationship problems occur, you address them in this way. Yet, you have not considered that the problem is the initial purpose you assigned to the relationship and that the experience of an empty present moment is a misperception.

I ask you to go back to the beginning of the interaction when you first experienced the emptiness. How you respond to the perceived lack determines how you relate to the person, place, or thing. The lack seems very real to you. I am not suggesting that you deny the experience of lack or ignore the need. I am not suggesting that the need is not something you deserve. Your experience in this world is meant to be one of pure love, joy, freedom, fulfillment, a sense of purpose, safety, and gratitude. I am saying this: It is your decision to receive these experiences from a person, place, or thing that must be changed.

All that you need, you already have. This idea seems crazy if you look at your hands and see they are empty. Yet, looking within yourself for what you lack is a decision you can make regardless of the evidence. It is only THIS decision that allows you to release the demands that you make on your relationships. If you try not to make demands while believing you do not have what you need, you set yourself up for disappointment. Putting forth just a little effort to turn within instead of making external demands is all you need to begin to heal your relationships.

Give yourself appreciation and gratitude for every effort you CAN make. You will not find this easy because you have been conditioned to use your relationships to get what you need. To return to the original purpose of experiencing pure love in all your relationships requires effort until you learn that you always have what you need in any present moment. That is why I am directing you to look within whenever you lack something you need. This easier way changes the purpose of your relationships. When you realize you have what you need, love will naturally take its rightful place as the ultimate reward of being in a relationship.

"Thank you."

April 3

You experience the ebb and flow of your relationships as either a source of pain or a way to freedom. Some people like the idea that relationships come into their lives and then flow out because this idea allows them to exit relationships whenever they become uncomfortable. Others dislike the idea that relationships are not necessarily forever because they use their relationships to remind them that they are never alone. Therefore, there are two different responses to the endings of relationships. Some can easily let them go, while others struggle when relationships end.

Those who easily let them go do so because if there were no end to relationships, they would feel trapped in their discomfort. Some feel a deep sadness when they part ways because they believe relationships must stay intact to avoid experiencing loss. These two opposing ways of responding to the natural ebb and flow of relationships are neither "good" nor "bad" because both responses result from a general lack of understanding about relationships.

I am making a point to clarify how the world views relationships to move beyond this level of understanding to higher ground. From a spiritual viewpoint, two things happen simultaneously when you experience the ebb and flow of relationships. The most important thing to know is that your true relationship with all aspects of creation remains in a constant flow of unity. When one becomes aware of this union, any discussion about the ebb and flow of relationships is pointless because, in truth, there is no ebb, only flow. For those unaware of the truth and experiencing the beginnings and endings of relationships, there is a teaching that can help you use these experiences to reach higher ground.

You experience an ebb and flow of relationships, or so it seems. Consider all the relationships you had as a child, young adult, and as an adult. Even if you remain in someone's life for years, your relationship has undergone many changes. Even in a life-long relationship, your interactions vary. For today's teaching, let us focus on the relationships that have changed over the years.

From an earthly perspective, you experience the change in the following ways:

- You are no longer physically present in someone's life.

- You are physically present, yet you no longer feel the same way about this person.

- You are physically present and continue to love this person, yet you no longer share the same values, beliefs, or interests.

- You are physically present, your love is continual, and you share values, beliefs, and interests, yet you no longer have an intimate connection.

Whether the relationship stays or goes depends on whether you are someone who maintains the relationship to avoid feeling lonely or if you are someone who moves on from a relationship to avoid feeling uncomfortable.

Instead of desiring or resisting the beginning and ending of relationships, I offer you a third option: Allow love to be experienced in both the beginnings and endings of all your relationships. Some find this easier to do initially and challenging to do at the end. Others find it difficult to open their heart initially and find it easier to experience the fullness of love at the end. Which one is it for you?

Your answer correlates to how you respond to the ebb and flow of relationships. If you find it difficult to open your heart at the beginning and easier to love at the end, chances are you let go of relationships to avoid feeling uncomfortable. If it is easier to love in the beginning than it is at the end, chances are you hold onto relationships to avoid feeling the loss of love.

Allowing yourself to experience love at the beginning AND end helps you avoid the unhealthy response of clinging to or discarding the relationship. When love is present during the ebb and flow of relationships, you are more willing to let Divine wisdom bring you what you need and release what has served you well yet is no longer needed. Once you have accepted this third option as a valuable response to the beginning and end of relationships, you can ask for Divine help to achieve success.

I ask you to consider a relationship you would like to have or one that has ended. Contemplate and write down all that you are grateful for, whether at the beginning or the end of the relationship. This relationship will bring or has brought you many blessings. When you acknowledge all the gifts you will receive or have received from this interaction, you instantly experience the energy of love. Once this love is experienced, the beginning or end of the relationship becomes part of the flow of this loving energy.

"Thank you."

April 4

Today's message is a continuation of yesterday's teaching.

I am teaching you steps that lead to an expanded awareness of all that exists within consciousness. These steps contain markers that point to the truth. For instance, when you perceive love both in the beginning and at the end of a relationship, you are unifying what appears to be two separate events into one experience of love. Can you see how this practice points you toward the truth?

The opposite of this practice is treating each relationship differently and having numerous experiences throughout the relationship. You react, feel, and think differently depending on the type of relationship and how the other person responds. These differences create a disjointed experience that points you away from the truth. You might be tempted to disregard the practices I give you because they do not seem to be practices that will result in the ultimate experience of oneness. Consider this question: If you find it difficult to honor every relationship by allowing a unified experience of love when the relationship changes, how can you be open to knowing you are one with all creation?

Knowing where you are headed and the goal you want to achieve does not necessarily mean you are ready to welcome success. Each step you are willing to take prepares you for the ultimate experience. Be assured that your efforts are leading you toward achieving your goal.

Relationships in this world are a major stumbling block you trip over time and time again. All interactions have the potential to unify your world because, within the interaction, you can experience one feeling, one thought, and one perception. Yet, many interactions result in experiencing the opposite of love, oneness, and Divine truth. That is because when something appears apart from you, it is tempting to blame this "separate part" of existence for your unhappiness.

What brings you together initially is the potential to experience Divine love. Deep down, you know this experience is possible. That is why you are drawn to experience relationships while living in this world. When the interaction begins, you can experience glimpses of the love that unifies. Yet you also might become aware of unloving thoughts, perceptions, and feelings. This awareness can cause you to stumble and fall into an experience opposite of what you truly desire.

The potential to experience the love that unifies two seemingly separate parts is still great. At the moment when you stumble, however, it seems impossible. Keep the faith. At this precise moment, you can make an important decision that will determine your next present-moment experience. You can use the interaction to reexperience the love that unifies or use the interaction to reinforce the unloving feelings, thoughts, and perceptions that separate.

Deciding to experience unity and love, regardless of what you currently think, feel, and see, is a major step toward experiencing the ultimate truth of who you are. Do not minimize this opportunity by judging the decision as unimportant and seeing this interaction as inconsequential to achieving your spiritual goal. What might seem like a small practice to you is actually the work of a master student. You are challenging yourself to use even the most difficult circumstances to experience an expanded awareness of unity and Divine love.

Each interaction, whether at the beginning, middle, or end of the relationship, can help you take giant leaps toward your goal. When you feel the most challenged in relationships and are willing to practice these teachings, thank yourself. What you are willing to do on behalf of your peace of mind, you do for the world. Be assured that the whole world will benefit from your efforts.

"Thank you."

April 7

As I listen to a guided meditation titled "Oneness with God," tears spring to my eyes. Instead of being uplifted to a state of joy, I am overwhelmed by profound sadness. These feelings are reminiscent of the emotions I experienced when my past relationships ended. I turn on the recorder, eager to receive clarification and relief.

Note: I am instructed to place this message after the entry on April 4th.

The ending of a relationship, whether through death or because you have decided to go your separate ways, can trigger a memory of loss so devastating that you have buried it in an effort to try not to remember. The trauma of losing your spiritual home and your relationship with all creation and your Creator is the real source of your grief. This more profound "loss" is hardly ever recognized while living in this world, and it need not be. The remedy for healing the grief experienced at the end of a relationship in this world is the same remedy for healing your sense of separation from your Creator.

If you recognize that relationships have no beginning and no end, healing will happen instantly. The "grieving process" lasts as long as the sense of separation continues. The instant you are reunited, the pain is gone. Is this not so? I have said before that relationships are not physical. Your relationships are connections through an invisible bond that can never be broken. If you expand your awareness to this level of existence and experience your true relationship, the sadness disappears. Achieving this awareness while you believe you live in this world and experience yourself as a physical being is challenging.

The difficulty with accepting this remedy is your insistence that relationships have to do with the physical form. It is crucial not to pretend that you are ready for an answer when you are not. There is an answer that can free you from grief instantly, yet it requires a release of your current self-concept and the self-concept of the one you are in a relationship with. If you are not ready to let go, accepting the remedy might be seen as a double loss.

If this is the case, take comfort in knowing there is a remedy that will bring you happiness. Your task is to grow to be open to receiving the remedy. Love yourself while you grow to learn that this remedy is the answer you want. In the meantime, allow yourself to feel all that the present moment contains and, simultaneously, give permission for the Spirit of love to free you from pain. In this way, you honor your current experience without judging it and allow your experience to change without controlling it. The answer you are given will be the perfect remedy for you at the time. Trust that any remedy to ease your pain is a step closer to the ultimate realization of unity.

I offer you a way to use the life experience of relationships ending to heal the perception of your separation from the Source of all life. When these steps lead to the realization that you are one with your Creator and all of creation, you will be grateful for everything that led you to this joyful awareness. Until then, let Divine love love you where you are.

"Thank you."

April 5

I have pointed out that you are in a relationship in every present moment because you interact with the present moment through emotions, thoughts, and perceptions. Although this is true, we now must direct your learning toward how YOU define relationships.

You classify relationships as an experience you have with another person. You categorize relationships based on length of time and structure of hierarchy, which includes parent and child, boss and employee, teacher and student, grandparent and grandchild. Suppose there is an equal status such as acquaintances, friends, intimate partners, colleagues, and teammates. In that case, you subcategorize these relationships based on how strongly you feel connected, how much you care for them, and how deep the love is that you feel. Each relationship is unique in your eyes. Each relationship has its own set of problems and rewards. Therefore, you have plenty of opportunities to apply these teachings to various situations you encounter while interacting with others.

There is not one set of teachings for each type of relationship you have. There is one teaching that, when applied to every relationship, will give you one result. Yet, the various relationships you form in this world contain unique challenges that can derail your practice, thus delaying the rewards. For instance, a brief encounter with an acquaintance seems to have fewer challenges than a life-long relationship with a parent. You might find it easier to connect with a stranger and feel deep love than to connect with someone who has been in your life since birth. That is because a life-long relationship changes its structure and category many times over the years.

As time passes, each person in the relationship experiences many different emotions, thoughts, and perceptions. In contrast, a five-minute encounter with a stranger usually contains only one emotion, thought, and perception. This experience of the encounter can be anything you choose to feel, think, or perceive. If you are in a loving mindset when you meet a stranger or acquaintance, you feel happy, think good thoughts, and perceive a friendly face. If your mindset is negative when you cross paths with a stranger or acquaintance, you feel irritated, your thoughts are less than favorable, and you perceive someone disturbing your peace. The relationship does not last long enough for this experience to go through any changes.

Now consider how many of these interactions you have with someone who has been in your life for years. And then, consider how many different mindsets you have throughout one day. Is it any wonder that a life-long relationship presents unique challenges that a brief encounter does not? You might not enjoy the interaction with a stranger or acquaintance, yet this does not trouble you because you have already moved on to the next interaction.

A relationship involving many interactions presents you with a valuable opportunity to enrich your present-moment experience. Because this person will be with you in the next moment, you are motivated to use the interactions to experience greater happiness, freedom, and love. All relationships can be used for this purpose, yet the ones that last longer than a moment increase your desire to achieve the ultimate goal. Once you realize success, it is effortless to experience what you desire with a total stranger.

In a previous message (March 27th), I provided a practice to increase your awareness of all that is present in the moment you are in. This same practice can be used in your relationships:

+ Notice your emotions, thoughts, and perceptions without judgment.

+ Avoid analyzing others' intentions, feelings, and thoughts, which will only delay awareness of your own.

+ Be aware of the temptation to believe that what you are interacting with, whether a person, place, or thing, must change for your emotions, thoughts, and perceptions to change.

  ⬦ You can resist this temptation by simply returning your awareness to your feelings, thoughts, and perceptions.

+ See how long you can maintain this awareness without trying to change anything.

I will add one more step for relationships to help you achieve your goal.

Because the interaction is with a person versus a place or thing, it is important to be honest about what you are feeling, thinking, and perceiving at the moment. If you feel it is safe to do so, share with an open heart. The purpose of sharing is not to burden the other with the responsibility to change your emotions, thoughts, and perceptions. The purpose of sharing is to break down the false barriers that seem to separate you from another aspect of yourself.

When you share without making demands, you honor their presence in your life and encourage them to be honest with themselves. When this sharing is done in the spirit of unity and love while taking full responsibility for your own experiences, the barriers that seem to separate you melt away. Now, you can cross the bridge to a more expanded awareness of your true relationship with all creation.

"What if the other person will not receive what you share with an open mind and heart?"

If you are in a situation of extreme projection involving physical or emotional negative responses, I advise you to disengage from the interaction and practice the teachings I have given you. You are never alone in the present moment. You can share with your inner spirit (teachers, ascended masters, guides, higher self) and let this relationship guide you toward healing.

If the situation is conducive to sharing, speak from your heart without needing the other person to respond in a particular way. Remember, the purpose of sharing is not to agree but to open your heart through honesty—meaning you must be clear about your purpose. If you are secretly engaging in honesty to judge, make guilty, attack, defend, or elevate yourself, you have forgotten the reason why you share. If you cannot share without these goals, I would advise you to be quiet and ask for Divine help in accepting the only purpose that will lead to peace.

It is very difficult not to make demands on the world to give you what you need in the present moment. This difficulty arises when you have not yet realized your ability to look within and discover the abundance of experiences available to you in the present moment. If you stumble, that's okay. To steady yourself and avoid falling into an experience you do not want, practice the way I have given you. Practice is needed until you have perfected the skill. Be grateful for all the relationships in your life that provide so many opportunities to practice.

"Thank you."

April 6

Practicing honesty is an important step to experiencing expanded awareness in the present moment. And, practice, you must. It can be challenging to be honest with yourself and others in a loving, non-judgmental, and responsible way. If you are willing to practice honesty in all your relationships, you are taking a giant leap toward achieving the ultimate goal. However, if you mistake what you are honest about as the ultimate truth, you might lose more than you gain.

There is a tendency to believe that if you feel, think, and perceive a certain way, that is the way it is. This rigidity can cause you to stumble in your commitment to honesty. Always, always, always be willing to question your emotions, thoughts, and perceptions. To believe that your limited viewpoint is correct is to block greater wisdom, deeper love, and guidance that aligns with your purpose. Honesty, combined with an open mind, equals true freedom. Allowing yourself to fully feel the emotion, become aware of the thoughts, and acknowledge what you are perceiving is an excellent first step. Yet, unless you have an understanding that fosters love and compassion for yourself and others, you cannot claim that your experience is a fact. Until then, there is always room to expand your awareness to feel, think, and perceive differently.

A simple way to be honest and remain open-minded is to express what you currently feel, think, and perceive while asking for a change of heart and mind. You know the difference between love and fear, judgment and acceptance, attack and defenselessness, and hate and helpfulness. Therefore, you can discern when you need a change of mind and heart. Use this skill wisely because honesty combined with rigidity will delay your peace and rob you of joy. Honesty, combined with an open mind and a willingness to change, can reward you in ways you cannot even imagine.

Your relationships are the training ground to reach amazing heights of awareness. They are the means to move quickly ahead in the race to the finish line. At mile five, ten, fifteen, and so on, you might have difficulty recommitting to finishing the race. These are the moments in relationships when you question whether the goal is worth pursuing. These moments require more vigilance, determination, and trust. It is at these precise moments that you will find my teachings and practices the most helpful.

These relationship practices are given for you to enjoy every moment you are in. They have the power to change your current experience from one of fear and pain to love and joy. Your willingness to use these practices in your relationships is a beautiful gift you give to yourself and others. Do not be dismayed if you stumble or even fall. Ask for Divine help, accept what is given, and you will be lifted to expand your view of your relationship. THIS is how you love the world and love yourself. THIS is how your relationships become the means to experience heaven on earth.

"Thank you."

PART IV
Special Topics

Do not limit the questions you ask for fear that you are limiting our answers.

It is the act of asking that naturally opens you to receiving what you need.

MY SPIRIT GUIDES

Change

"This morning, I experienced something very unpleasant. I want to practice these teachings, but instead, I find myself frantically thinking of external solutions that will change this unpleasant experience into a pleasant one. What is helpful for us to understand when we have an intense desire to change our external experience because we are so uncomfortable?"

We are in a time of revolution from the confines of an old paradigm. Collectively, we are breaking free from the belief that it takes time to change our experience. This old paradigm was based on the premise that external circumstances regulate our experience. Transformation begins with the acceptance of what creates the experience. This acceptance is crucial to change.

If you want to change your experience without accepting a change of heart and mind, no real qualitative change will occur. When you are finally willing to feel and perceive something different, yet change still does not occur, you wonder why your experience does not change. This is because you have forgotten the fundamental ingredients that facilitate change.

When you try to change an experience while staying firmly rooted in your current level of consciousness, any movement you experience is tedious and tiresome. Even if you have learned that any change in form without a change in perception, thought, and feeling will be less than satisfying, you still have not acknowledged what, where, and how change occurs.

What needs to change is your awareness. Where change occurs is in a new level of consciousness. How this change happens is through the practices I have taught you. When you desire a change, remember that the change you seek is a movement from your current level of awareness to a higher level of consciousness.

Here are steps you can take to facilitate this change:

1. You are free to examine your current level of consciousness fully. This exploration can include awareness of negative or positive feelings and a full, detailed story about what is happening and why. Although this step is unnecessary, you might find it helpful to be honest about your current experience as a way to become aware of your desire for change and why you might resist change.

2. To help you remember what needs to change for your experience to be different, visualize a bridge that will carry you from one level of consciousness to another.

3. Express your willingness to leave everything behind for something new. THIS decision leads to real change.

4. Then, be open to receiving whatever you are ready for. Do not prejudge what you will receive. It can be a feeling, direction, action, understanding, awareness, or healing of an old pattern—anything that offers a loving solution to your current experience.

A clinging can occur in a moment of change, which is perfectly normal. Even though you truly desire a change in experience, you might resist letting go of your current view of the world, which includes your current self-concept. Try not to judge yourself and slip back into old patterns that keep you from growing. It is okay to feel uncomfortable when trying new things. To help you keep your focus on what, where, and how real change occurs, revisit the image of the bridge and then let your mind expand naturally.

To properly assess if a change is occurring, focus on your internal experience throughout the day and notice any positive changes. These are the indicators that real qualitative change is happening. This internal shift will have a ripple effect in the external world. Note these changes as well. They are less important, yet they teach you that you deserve happiness and freedom no matter what level of consciousness you are experiencing.

"Thank you."

Manifestation

"There is a general understanding that through manifestation, we can change an unpleasant external experience to one that is more desirable. What would you share regarding using the practice of manifestation to get what we want?"

Manifestation is a natural law of cause and effect. It begins with desire and ends with results. However, when you are only aware of the desire and refuse to acknowledge what motivates the desire, you can experience disappointment even if you get what you want.

Your desire to have certain experiences can originate from a lower-based or higher vibrational energy. In other words, your desires can be motivated through fear, guilt, sacrifice, confusion about what is helpful or hurtful, and your strict rules of "right" and "wrong." Lower-based desires can also be motivated by the need to escape. For instance, a strong desire to experience a new relationship can originate from the fear of being alone. A desire for a new career might arise from the need to escape the feeling of inadequacy experienced in your current position. A desire for financial freedom can be motivated by a belief that you are not safe and, therefore, need to stockpile savings to feel secure.

On the other hand, these desires can be motivated through love, innocence, worthiness, willingness to feel all emotions fully, and openness to attune to what is right for you. If these are your motivations, the manifestation of the desire for a relationship, financial freedom, or a new career will lead to joy.

Not all desires lead to joy. I tell you this so you do not blindly follow all of your desires to full manifestation. I ask you to look deeply into the desire and explore what lies beneath it.

I see an image of an iceberg.

Your willingness to explore what motivates the desire is a gift you give to yourself. No matter what you discover, you have the means to heal all lower-based energies driving you away from happiness and love. When you no longer try to fix or run from these lower-based energies, your desires will naturally align with the higher vibrations of love, worthiness, and true connection.

When you find that your desires are motivated through a higher vibration, trust these desires and follow them to fruition. If you encounter delays, look deeply into what fears and beliefs you have carried with you. Maybe you fear others will be hurt if you pursue your desire. Maybe you believe you are undeserving of this new experience. If you encounter lower-based thoughts, ask for Divine help in sorting out what is true.

Love is your guiding light and will help you discern what drives your desires. Love is always trying to lead you toward joy and away from pain. If you are divinely guided to let go of a desire, you might begin to feel these lower-based energies. Resist the temptation to run from these uncomfortable emotions and beliefs. What you genuinely want is a release from what motivates you to pursue desires that are not in your best interest. Be willing to explore what is beneath the surface of the desire. Ask to be free from what keeps you running in circles and never reaching your heart's true desire. Love will release you from these lower-based energies with your permission. Then, when you experience the higher vibrational energies, you will know your heart's true desires. Trust these desires. They will lead you to joy.

"When we have a strong desire to leave an uncomfortable or dissatisfying situation, can this desire be motivated through a higher vibration?"

You seek to experience greater happiness and freedom while living in this world. That is a worthy goal. I am teaching you how to find what you seek.

I spoke about the motivation to change coming from lower-based or higher vibrational energies. That does not mean you will always FEEL the higher vibrations of love, peace, and joy when these energies motivate you to make a change. Love can motivate you to make a change because it is advantageous for you in reaching your goal of expansion and growth. Yet, you might feel uncomfortable, dissatisfied, and anxious.

Regardless of what motivates you to change, all changes can be helpful because you are aware, and awareness is the key to knowing yourself. You are quick to judge your wants and needs, and this judgment leads you away from freedom and happiness. Therefore, I advise against judgment and encourage you to love all experiences, even dissatisfaction and the desire for change. This response will enable you to find what is most helpful for you in the moment when you judge.

When you notice a desire to change, try to remain in your current condition for a brief moment and remember your purpose: Your greatest happiness and freedom is attained through the experience of true love for yourself and others and an inner awareness of peace, joy, safety, comfort, and unity. When you feel sure of your goal, ask what next step will lead you closer to your goal. You might experience internal shifts while remaining in your current surroundings. You might feel the natural desire to move from one situation to another. Trust and follow these urges to change. When you are aligned with the natural energy of love, what is manifested will bring you great joy.

All changes are helpful when you accept that the change can clear your mind of any fear, guilt, unworthiness, separation, and unloving thoughts that you still cling to. A change can help you recognize the love, joy, and peace available to you at any given moment. If you accept this help when you make the change, you can experience the freedom and joy you seek. The difference is that you will know exactly HOW you manifested the joy, peace, and love you experience.

"Thank you."

Abundance

"I feel immense gratitude for the love and care of family and friends and the gentle flow of daily life. In the past, I experienced forms of lack and struggled with my purpose and value. What would you share regarding the experiences of lack and abundance?"

Imagine being born into a rich family and living cooperatively in an abundant community. You have everything you want and all that you need. This experience is all you know; therefore, to you, it is the only reality that exists. For you, it is natural to live in a world that provides the essentials you need to live a gentle, joyful life. Living with ease and grace, you give effortlessly to those around you, and they give back to you in the same spirit of joy. All is given and received effortlessly because you all live in an abundant universe. Experiencing your natural state of being, it would never occur to you that an alternative experience exists. You would not understand lack of any kind because it is not part of your world. If you were asked to describe your abundant reality, you would say that it is an experience of your natural state of being.

Now, imagine you have wandered away from home. The years pass by. You have forgotten where you came from and what your life was like before you wandered off into the unknown. You have a distant memory of having everything you need and experiencing a life of gentleness and joy. In your current view, however, you struggle to make ends meet, and it seems as if there is not enough to sustain you. This distant memory of living with grace and ease helps you to strive for an experience where you struggle less and enjoy life more. Without this distant memory of your natural state of being, you would accept your current version of reality and not want something different. Thank God you can remember the life you were born to live.

Now, let us return to your question regarding the experiences of lack and abundance. In the analogy, you experience a lack when you are away from your true home. You experience abundance when you live in your natural state of being. Yet, you can never be away from home. Therefore, you always live in an abundant universe.

I am being reminded of the elevator analogy.

When you are in the present moment, and your view of reality is limited to the four walls, you do not see your true home. You view a world that seems to have taken you far from home. You conclude that you must have wandered off and now lack what you need. Actually, you remain in your true home and have closed your eyes to what exists all around you. Therefore, to change your experience from one of lack to one of abundance, you merely need to open your spiritual eyes to see and feel what is already there. It is a purely energetic, invisible experience of abundance that, for the moment, has not yet taken form. As you allow your awareness to expand to include Divine love, innocence, and unity, your internal experience will be expressed and reflected in the world.

The biggest challenge when you experience lack is your belief that it is a lack in form. All your efforts are directed toward solving the problem of lack with physical things. Adding fear to the moment increases your efforts to get things in the world to help you feel safe. I would advise you to use a gentle approach when challenged in this way. Remind yourself that your desire to experience a life of gentleness, ease, and joy comes from a memory of your natural state of being. Your desire to live an abundant life is the same as your desire to remember who you are and where you came from. Therefore, both are worthy goals.

Notice that your current view of reality or level of consciousness involves certain feelings, thoughts, and perceptions. Turning your attention inward will help you focus on the invisible experience of lack. Acknowledge and accept that your greatest need at this moment is to experience Divine love, perceive innocence and unity, and feel joy. You lack awareness of these precious gifts. Ask to experience these gifts now.

Observe how your world becomes brighter as it fills with reflections of your natural state of being. These changes in your world are not occurring because you changed the four walls or left the present moment to return home. Your world is changing because you are opening your eyes.

"Thank you."

Love

The world's concept of love is not what love is. This confusion about love is why many experience unhappiness and pain while living in this world.

Your experiences reflect a definition of love that includes ideas such as giving to get, sacrifice, compromise, selflessness, and suffering. You experience love as an emotion that can change. You feel love when the conditions are favorable and lose that loving feeling when conditions have changed. Therefore, love is experienced only when the conditions are right. If someone acts a certain way, meets your needs, and generally helps you feel good about yourself, you feel love. If behaviors change, needs go unmet, or you feel inadequate, unworthy, or undeserving, you lose that loving feeling. According to the world's definition, love is an internal feeling that you control.

There are many other examples in this world of the ebb and flow of "love" that you experience. Suffice it to say that "love" becomes a great source of disappointment and pain, not because love hurts but because you have misunderstood love. When you have these experiences while living in this world, it is best not to equate them with love. If you do, you will not seek the experience of real love.

I see an image of a field of grass. When I look below the surface, I see layers and layers of roots and dirt deep underground.

The surface of the grass is a symbol of the world's definition of love. It is exposed to the elements and, therefore, can change. What lies beneath the surface is real love—protected and nurtured and, therefore, never changes. If you stay on the surface, you will forever be chasing the feeling of love because the world's version of love is fleeting. It is given and then quickly taken away. You will try to catch it and hold onto it by any means available. You will play a game of hide and seek without ever winning.

Real love is something you can find and keep. It is constant and available to you in any moment. Because this love is at the root of all living things, it can be experienced anywhere, at any time, regardless of what you or others do, say, or think. Whether you discover it, however, depends on where you are looking for it.

Recall a moment when you felt the absence of love. Imagine that you are standing in a field of grass, looking around for the love that you lost. Now, look down at your feet and realize that what you seek is beneath you and has been holding you the whole time. Whenever you experience an absence of love, it is because you believe it is something else and somewhere else. In these moments of confusion, disappointment, and pain, remember what it is you seek and where it can be found.

There is no need to strain or struggle to discover real love. Rest, redefine what love is, and redirect your focus. These three actions are all you need to do to experience real love.

"Thank you."

Doubt

I had a dream the night before I received this message. In the dream, an enormous sky stretches from one end of the horizon to the other. In the middle of the vast sky is a small circle. Written inside the circle is the word "doubt." I sense that I need to pay attention to this word because, somehow, focusing on doubt aids in the continued expansion of the sky. The next morning, I write down the dream message and turn on the recorder. I am eager to learn how doubt is relevant to expansion.

I see the word "love," indicating a message coming through.

When you are uncertain and lack conviction in any endeavor, you hesitate to continue. As a consequence, you do not reap the rewards. When you are uncertain and lack conviction while practicing these teachings, you return to your old ways, thereby limiting your awareness and denying yourself joy.

Let's pause for a moment and see if you can glimpse the experience of joy.

I pause and focus on experiencing joy. I can't quite fully capture it. However, I do feel twinges of excitement and delight.

Imagine what it would be like to feel elated and free in every moment. Joy is a marvelous experience that closely reflects your true state of being. When you experience joy while living in this world, you are on the brink of knowing yourself as a pure Divine spirit. When you have difficulty applying these teachings and practices, it is not because you doubt whether they will be effective. You waver in your practice because you doubt that you want the experience these teachings and practices offer you.

Consider a situation where it is difficult for you to apply these teachings. Feel the experience fully and include all of your emotions and all of your thoughts. Now imagine that you are in the same situation, and you suddenly feel joyful. Can you imagine this change with little effort, or are you resistant to experiencing joy while remaining in the situation? If you can easily imagine a shift of this magnitude, then you are clear about what you desire. If you are resistant to your experience shifting from distress to joy while the situation stays the same, you need Divine help to recognize what you want.

You are conditioned to believe that happiness and freedom are gained through a change in form. Form DOES change. That is why you would feel unstable most of the time if your happiness depended on it. In contrast, experiencing internal joy, strength, and peace allows you to move freely without losing your balance.

To aid you in accepting rather than resisting the gift of constant joy, examine what you hope to gain when it is difficult for you to apply these teachings. Conduct this examination in the spirit of love, not judgment. You are willing to look deeper into the resistance and discover what holds you back from experiencing joy. What a wonderful gift you are giving to yourself.

Once you have a list of possible gains, notice how you believe each change in form will provide you with safety, happiness, and peace of mind. If they do provide these things, I assure you it is only temporary because form changes. And what they provide is nothing like the experience of pure joy, complete safety, and unwavering peace that these teachings and practices offer you. You cannot know the truth of this statement without the experience. Therefore, it is best to let Divine wisdom be in charge of deciding what you want. This surrender practice is an excellent anecdote to your doubt. The only effort that is required from you is your willingness to be led.

When you are in a situation you do not like, say, "I do not know what I need or want in this situation. I am open to Divine guidance." Notice any thoughts, feelings, perceptions, directions, or actions that come to mind. You might be led to look at an old pattern. You might suddenly gain a new understanding of the situation. You might be guided to make an external change. You might be directed toward a particular person, place, or resource. You might spontaneously experience love for everyone involved. The response from Divine wisdom will vary depending on your needs. Trust and follow the guidance you receive. When you reap the rewards, you will know beyond a reasonable doubt that what you received is what you've always wanted.

"Thank you."

Concluding
Messages

The core of all spiritual teachings,
if their purpose is to teach truth,
is to lead the student to a place of acceptance where
they willingly admit they know nothing at all.

In this glorious moment of uncertainty and confusion,
the thoughts of separation cease.

And now, the truth can be revealed and understood.

MY SPIRIT GUIDES

The Power of Love

I see the word "love."

I am showing you the word "love" at the end as I did in the beginning. You will notice that love is the main teaching throughout these practices and understandings. You will recognize that you have understood these teachings by the experiences you have when you practice. Regardless if you enter the present moment in distress or peace, the teachings and practices will expand your awareness to such heights that your experience of every present moment will be joyful. If your practice results in continued despair, you have forgotten its primary purpose. You have found a way to use your practice to continue to judge yourself or others. If this occurs, find it in your heart to replace judgment with love. To continue to judge yourself or others for denying yourself or others love is counterproductive and will result in delays.

I have taught you that the power to change your internal experience is in your own hands. Do not confuse power with force. When you force your will on another or yourself, you do so because you are in fear. When you utilize your inherent power to decide what you want to experience and then allow a change in feeling, thought, and perception, you learn the power of love.

Learn to be motivated to change your current experience by love rather than fear or upset. When you are distressed in your present moment, you are highly motivated to change your experience. It is your opportunity to learn of your power and the precious gift a change of mind and heart can offer you. This learning is essential and can help you take the steps necessary to reach your ultimate goal. Expanded awareness, however, contains experiences of love that stretch beyond the limitations that occur when love is constricted to fit into the level of third-dimensional consciousness you call the world.

Once you are comfortable with experiencing love in this world through your practice of greeting each present moment with a willingness to change, you can quickly cross the bridge to experience the next level of love. Each time you cross a bridge into a more expanded level of consciousness, you experience greater love and happiness than you did while resting in the previous level of awareness. If you cross the first bridge from distress to love and continue to expand your awareness, there will be no more distress—only more and more love.

When you find yourself going back and forth between distress and love, you are creating a new habit of response. This internal movement will result in a happier life. Once this response becomes a habit, consider what you might be missing when crossing the bridge only to return to distress. Greater happiness, freedom, and love await your arrival at the next level of consciousness. Each bridge you cross is the beginning of another bridge that will expand your awareness of all that exists in the present moment.

When you find that most of your present-moment experiences are peaceful, do not be tempted to go back to experiencing distress to motivate yourself to keep growing spiritually. Remain in a state of peace and use this level of experience as a springboard to greater awareness. Capture the wonderment of a child who looks at the nighttime sky and wonders what lies beyond the moon and the stars. There is more to see and feel even in a peaceful present moment, and it's all good.

As you gain greater understanding through these teachings and use these practices in the present moment, continue to ask, "What lies beyond this experience? Is there more to see, think, and feel in this present moment?" When you ask these questions, you expand your view of the present moment and remain open to new and surprising insights.

"Thank you."

Experiencing Heaven on Earth

You asked me to help you learn how to use your life experiences to gain greater freedom, happiness, and a sense of unity while living in this world. You were drawn to me because of the peace, love, freedom, and joy that I am experiencing. Deep inside, you know it is possible to be in this world and experience this amazing state of being. This state is referred to as an experience of heaven on earth. Anyone who believes this experience is possible will seek the means to make it happen. Many do not believe that their life here can reflect their life in their true home. They believe they must wait for their rewards as a child of God. All desired experiences are honored. There is no judgment. Yet, there is no reason to delay your happiness.

Anyone who walks the world in a spiritual state of pure love, freedom, and joy reminds us that God gives us everything now. Reaching this state while living in this world requires a particular form of practice that is not useful to those willing to wait. For those who believe they can have freedom now and are willing to use their life experiences as a means to freedom, these teachings and practices can be beneficial. When you reach this state of being through your commitment, determination, and vigilance, you encourage others not to delay.

A spiritual journey is a personal one. And yet, one's personal journey has universal significance. Whatever path you choose is up to you. You know what is right for you. Remember, you are always leading yourself. Never judge another's chosen path, and at the same time, know that what you choose for yourself can contribute to the lives of others. My teachings and practices are given as an answer to your request. Your request comes from a deeper knowledge of what you need to achieve your ultimate goal. Even though these individual choices seem only to serve you, trust me when I tell you that ALL will benefit from your choice. Follow the path that is right for you and you will learn the truth of this statement.

Life is given for you to experience beauty, joy, and love. Thank you to all who are willing to explore life's experiences to their fullest and receive greater freedom, happiness, and joy now.

"Thank you."

One Last Question . . .

"My willingness to receive your messages was motivated by my long-ing to experience freedom and joy and to serve others. What would be helpful for me to understand before the messages are shared?"

I would like you to know that your willingness to listen and ask questions has been most helpful in sharing what I know with those who want to learn. Sometimes, the desire to deepen what you know is not enough to bypass the interference to listening. We have joined together to honor the desire of your heart and to answer the call others make to help them learn how to be free now. Our efforts to provide a path home will make a difference in the lives of others and in your own life.

Please remember the essential teaching that makes this path a gentle one: Honor everyone's chosen path while encouraging everyone to choose a way home that is gentle and loving. Many deeply long to experience their true home but have forgotten that they deserve to be free of distress and fear each step of the way. If you remind just one person of their right to be free and they claim it for themselves, you have been truly helpful while helping yourself. I remind you of the first message I gave you: Love is why you listen and share. When you remember this essential teaching, you continue to share in the spirit of love.

Your intentions are at the heart of everything you do, say, think, or feel. If your intention is love and true helpfulness, then you can be assured that the energy that carries the messages to the world will be loving. That is all you need to know. How the messages are received and used, or not used, is nothing to be concerned about.

I see this image: I open my hands, and tiny, colorful butterflies fly into the air.

Freely receive. Freely give.

"Thank you."

With my eyes still closed, I see the butterfly image fade into the background. I somehow know the next and final image will be the name of my spirit guide. My heart races in anticipation. Nervously, I ask, "Please give me the individual letters instead of the word to ensure the accuracy of the name." As each letter appears, I speak the letter into the recorder.

N-e-s-h-e-a.

I speak his name out loud. "Neshea. Neshea." My heart is full.

I turn off the recorder. The interview is complete. My life will never be the same.

Neshea's Final Words

"I want to honor all that you have given to us by making sure that the messages are what you would share. Should I conduct a review process?"

We will work together to ensure that the messages are precise and clear. Keep in mind that if corrections are needed, they are made only to ensure that the one who wants to learn is given the teaching in the most helpful way. Do not add your own meaning to the review process, or you will deny yourself the joy of releasing the messages to the world. If you feel nervous during the review process, return to the first message and read it entirely. Remembering that your intentions are pure and loving; your concerns about the review process will disappear.

Process:

1. Please review each section with an open mind.

2. When a sentence seems unclear, highlight it, but do not make changes right away.

3. Read the section in its entirety and then return to the sentence.

4. Sit in silence, close your eyes, and ask to receive the words for that one sentence again.

   + The sentence might appear in your mind exactly as it is written.

   + There might be a few changes in the words or positioning of the words in the sentence.

   + The sentence might be deleted altogether or moved elsewhere.

"Should I do this review on my own?"

Yes. And at the same time, have a friend read the messages like I've outlined for you. Once they have highlighted any confusing sentence, sit in silence and ask for clarity. Make any necessary changes and then repeat the same process.

Do the work in the spirit of joy and love, just as you would be happy to put forth your energy and time toward preparing a meal or a party for a loved one.

I hear in my mind the tune "Whistle While You Work" from the movie Snow White and the Seven Dwarfs. *I find the lyrics on the Internet. The last two lines state that when you imagine your work as someone you love, you'll be so joyful that the time spent working will fly by.*

I smile as I recall my dream encounter with Neshea and his light-hearted, boyish charm. How fitting that Neshea's last instructions are given through a Disney song.

I then scribe Neshea's final words:

The experience of true love, present in every moment,
frees our minds and hearts to laugh, to love, and
to be a beacon of light for others.

"Thank you."

Reflections and Revelations

DIVINE GUIDANCE is not always recognized in the moment. Immersed in our daily tasks and challenges, it can take days, months, or years before we recognize and are grateful for the support we receive. For me, it wasn't until after a life-changing event and a global pandemic that I fully appreciated my time with Neshea and the messages he shared.

In *Freedom Now,* I write, "Some of life's events are familiar, and some moments are a complete surprise." A few weeks after scribing Neshea's final words, I learned how true that statement is. A family member's sudden debilitating illness uprooted my peaceful routine and threw me into a world of chaos. Abruptly leaving my home, I traveled to another state to help navigate the medical maze of specialists and treatments. Witnessing an illness I knew nothing about, I struggled to maintain a sense of calm. At times the fear, sadness, and panic were crippling. And then, the World Health Organization declared Covid-19 a global pandemic. What little was left of my routine and stability vanished. Disoriented and unable to read, pray, or meditate, I clung to the daily practice I had developed during my time with Neshea. In quiet moments and moments of distress, I honestly explored my thoughts, feelings, patterns of behavior, and perceptions and then asked for help from the spiritual realm. The insights and guidance I received eased the turmoil of daily life and led to moments of profound understanding and peace.

Four years later, it was time to prepare *Freedom Now* for publication. Dusting off the manuscript, I reread Neshea's teachings and had an epiphany. Even though I hadn't read a word of the manuscript since the Spring of 2019, I had been practicing its teachings and reaping the rewards. The premise of *Freedom Now* is that each present moment contains our fears and wisdom. And when we release the boundaries that block the awareness of both, we discover what we need to carry us through life's challenges. Looking back on the previous four years, I know this teaching is true. Realizing the magnitude of the gift I received from Neshea, the tears flowed.

The spiritual realm is not a figment of our imagination. Invisible helpers are real, and their support is vital to living a life with purpose and joy. Each day, I give thanks for the guidance and insights my spiritual dreams, visions, and channelings offer. Through Divine guidance, I'm learning to trust my journey and allow my soul to lead the way.

Thank You

A HEARTFELT thank you to Neshea, my spirit guide. Your teachings are a beacon of light, especially during challenging times. I am forever grateful for our dream encounter.

To the publishing team at Sunbury Press, thank you for your commitment to publishing channeled teachings. The world needs these fresh ideas and new perspectives. Your willingness to devote resources to sharing Neshea's messages helps create a peaceful and harmonious world.

To Chelsea, Maureen, Alyssa, Sandie, and Jessica—thank you for reading the daily transcripts and validating the teachings' relevancy and helpfulness. Your support and encouragement were essential to completing *Freedom Now*.

A special thank you to Cheryl, my dear friend and editor, for devoting countless hours to editing my notes and organizing the content of Neshea's messages. The moments spent together reviewing *Freedom Now* are cherished memories.

Lastly, I am grateful for everything in my life, including the challenges I've faced. In times of joy and despair, I've learned that I am never alone and deeply loved. This awareness of my connection to inner wisdom and love has made every moment precious to me.

References

A Course in Miracles Combined Volume. 2nd ed., 1975. Tiburon, CA: Foundation for Inner Peace, 1992.

A Course in Miracles: Complete & Annotated Edition. Edited by Robert Perry. West Sedona, AZ: Circle of Atonement, 2017.

Know thyself. Accessed November 21, 2022. https://en.wikipedia.org/wiki/Know_thyself

Fields, Patti. 2022. *A Guide to Aligning with the Source of Healing.* Rochester, New York. PDF

Return to Oneness–Self Healing Collective, "Oneness with God." *YouTube.* Online Video Clip, https://www.youtube.com/watch?v=CkS7U6dDd6k (accessed 7 April 2019).

Fields, Patti. 2022. *Special Instructions for the Role of the Healer.* Rochester, New York. PDF.

Fields, Patti. 2022. *A Guide to Communicating with the Spiritual Realm.* Rochester, New York. PDF.

Jalal ad-Din Muhammad Balkhi, 1207-1273 and Coleman. Barks.1996. *The Essential Rumi.* San Francisco, CA, Harper. Accessed November 7, 2022. https://www.azquotes.com/author/12768-Rumi?p=23.

Lyrics.com, STANDS4 LLC, 2019. "Whistle While You Work Lyrics." Accessed April 10, 2019. https://www.lyrics.com/lyric/17384080/Adriana+Caselotti.

About the Author

AFTER EXPERIENCING a devastating event, PATTI FIELDS' quest for answers led her to the teachings and practices of *A Course in Miracles*, during which time her dreams and visions became numerous and profound. Applying the spiritual messages she received to situations and relationships, her negative patterns, grievances, and unhealthy self-concepts fell away. As a result, Patti had truly miraculous experiences.

Patti's desire to help others prompted an unexpected dream where she met her spirit guide, Neshea, who taught her how to channel messages while awake. Since scribing Neshea's teachings, Patti has channeled several books that offer spiritual insights to universal questions and concerns. Patti's dreams, visions, and channeled messages have profoundly affected her life and she is passionate about sharing these teachings so others can benefit, too.

Connect with Patti on Instagram @patti_fields or check out her website at www.pattifields.com, where you can explore free resources and sign up to receive new channeled messages and Patti's free *Guide to Spiritual Dreaming*.

www.ingramcontent.com/pod-product-compliance
Lightning Source LLC
Chambersburg PA
CBHW011155090426
42740CB00018B/3394